# MIDTOWN BANK

## A Bank Teller Simulation

**Patsy Hall Sargent**
**Mary Faye Ward**

# BANK

**South-Western**
**Educational Publishing**

| | |
|---|---|
| Vice President/Editor-in-Chief: | Dennis Kokoruda |
| Managing Editor: | Carol Volz |
| Developmental Editor: | Mark D. Beck |
| Production Coordinator: | Carol Sturzenberger |
| Production Editor II: | Melanie A. Blair-Dillion |
| Senior Designer: | Elaine St. John-Lagenaur |
| Photo Editor: | Sam Marshall |

ISBN: 0-538-60267-8

2 3 4 5 6 7 8 9 H 04 03 02 01 00 99 98 97

Printed in the United States of America

*Photo credits:* p. 4, © 1993, Richard Younker; p. 30, American Express Company; p. 44, Diebold, Inc.; p. 55, Western Union; p. 59, © 1985, Dana L. Duke

I(T)P
International Thomson Publishing
South-Western Educational Publishing is an ITP Company. The ITP trademark is used under license.

# CONTENTS

# PREFACE

*MIDTOWN BANK: A Bank Teller Simulation* is a simulated on-the-job training course designed to give future money handlers, such as cashiers, bank tellers, and small business vendors, an opportunity to learn the mechanics involved in receiving, disbursing, and accounting for money. A financial institution setting was chosen because it is usually associated with honesty, integrity, and responsibility.

This simulation provides various avenues of instruction:

- An *Employee Manual* instructs students about bank documents, bank policy, and bank organization.

- Computer software allows students to use the latest technology to practice receiving, disbursing, and accounting for money.

- Human relations tips appear throughout the *Employee Manual* so students can learn about successful business dealings with others and their property.

- Interesting activities teach entry-level job skills that are used in various careers. These skills include handling checks and deposits, filing alphabetically and numerically, comparing signatures and identification documents, learning institutional policies (employee pay, work habits, and so on), using the computer keyboard and numeric keypad, understanding and using computer software, handling money with accuracy, and learning security procedures.

- Incentives teach students to perform at an exemplary level. A high level of performance provides bonus pay as well as pride in a job well done.

Students can work individually or in a group setting. The simulation is self-contained, self-instructional, and very readable. It can be incorporated easily into various high school, business school, and college courses.

An *Instructor's Manual* provides guidance in presenting the simulation to students, suggestions for adding variety to the learning experience, evaluation procedures, solutions to the student exercises and tests, and sample documents for duplication. The instructor will be in a supervisory position for the "bank employees" as they train and experience several days of bank teller work—a pleasant break from the regular routine.

The authors, Pat Sargent and Mary Faye Ward, are experienced high school and community college teachers with MBE degrees, business education certification, and vocational certification. They have studied the policies and practices of various banking institutions in order to make the simulation activities and forms realistic. *MIDTOWN BANK: A Bank Teller Simulation* also reflects the impact of the computer in the banking industry today.

The authors wish to thank all who helped to make this simulation a successful learning tool—various bankers, editors, and reviewers.

# WELCOME TO MIDTOWN BANK

There seems to be a commercial bank, credit union, or savings and loan association on nearly every corner or in every shopping center. Some banks are small, independent banks that are owned and operated at one location. Other banks are merely branches of large organizations that have numerous locations as well as a central office that provides various services for the branches.

Banks may seem a little mysterious. Employees don't talk much about what happens there; security is very tight. Sometimes a uniformed officer stands in the bank lobby.

You notice an ad in the classified section of the paper for a teller trainee job at Midtown Bank. (See Figure W.1.) You have heard that the bank has a number of branches at various locations in your city and you decide to investigate this career opportunity. You send a letter and resume (shown in Figure W.2), and are asked to go to the bank for an interview.

You learn that your keyboarding and computer literacy skills, your money handling experience in a previous job, and your interest in banking as a career are sufficient for an entry-level position at Midtown Bank. You have the job!

You are about to begin an exciting and satisfying learning experience that will prepare you for a cashiering (or bank teller) position. Your "on-the-job" training will be thorough and enjoyable. You will learn valuable skills that are fundamental in the world of business. These skills are important for any employee who works with money and, specifically, for employees who work in banks, savings institutions, and credit unions. These skills include:

**TELLER TRAINEE**

We are a large bank currently interviewing for a full-time Teller Trainee position. Individuals must be dependable and possess good communication skills. Prefer computer and cash handling experience. Good typing skills a plus. Please forward resume to:

Teller Trainee
P.O. Box 32109
Dallas, TX 75150

**Figure W.1**

*Classified Advertisement for Teller Trainee Position*

1. **Cashiering.** As a bank employee, you will receive customers' deposits and make disbursements. A cashiering position is designated differently in various localities and situations. Some common titles are sales representative, customer service representative, cashier, teller, and financial sales representative. At Midtown Bank, you will be called a **bank teller**. You will also balance a cash drawer at the end of the business day and route information to appropriate departments. You will learn about the proof department and understand how it affects your job as a teller.

Student Name
Student Address
Student City and State
Student Phone Number

EDUCATION
Valley Community College, September 19-- to May 19--:
Completed Introduction to Computers and Computer
Applications courses.

Valley High School, graduated May, 19--

WORK EXPERIENCE
19-- to Present    Allstar Sporting Goods. Clerk. Duties
included cashiering with computerized
register; handling cash, check, and credit
purchases; and maintaining inventory.

19-- to 19--       Goodtimes Yogurt. Part-time clerk. Duties
included waiting on customers, cashiering,
and balancing cash register drawer.

MEMBERSHIP AND HONORS
Future Business Leaders of America, Valley High
School – treasurer
Volunteer fundraiser for Food Pantry
Tennis letter, Valley High School, 2 years

REFERENCES
Provided on request.

2. **Computer Use.** In many banks, employees are able to access account information immediately by using a computer. The computer is on-line (direct communication through the computer system) with the central office, which includes the bookkeeping and proof departments of the institution. By using the specially designed Midtown Bank software, you will access customer account information, such as bank balances, customer addresses and telephone numbers, and so on, that is on file with the bank. You will also complete customer transactions and retrieve and give information to customers from the computer database.

3. **Bookkeeping.** You will learn about bank procedures, disburse and update information, and complete forms with proper data.

4. **Filing.** You will use basic alphabetic and numeric filing rules.

5. **Human Relations.** "Tips" like the one shown here will help you learn how to react pleasantly and efficiently to customer requests and complaints according to Midtown Bank policy. They will also give you ideas about how to cooperate with fellow employees in completing your daily tasks.

**HUMAN RELATIONS TIP**

Bank tellers must be courteous because they are the bank's representatives in dealing with its customers.

For the next few weeks, picture yourself as a new employee at the Second Avenue Branch of Midtown Bank in Dallas, Texas. Unit I will help you become acquainted with the policies of Midtown Bank. Follow the directions given as you continue through the units of instruction. Good luck in your training!

# ORIENTATION

## Objectives

At the completion of Unit I, you will be able to:

- Interpret a bank organization chart.
- Complete a timecard.
- Set up an electronic time log.
- Launch and navigate the menus of the Midtown Bank software.

# Beginning Your New Job

Today is your first day on the job at Midtown Bank. You have been asked to meet with the branch manager for an orientation session before you begin your duties as a teller trainee.

The manager tells you in general what it is like to work in a bank. You discuss some of the reasons banking is a challenging career:

1. Banks are people oriented. Banks employ people with various educational backgrounds, and these employees see many different people every day. The recurring challenge is to make customers glad that you and your bank are part of their lives.

> **HUMAN RELATIONS TIP**
>
> Bank employees like to meet and talk to people.

2. Banks offer many advantages to their employees. Banks pay average salaries and provide abundant opportunities for advancement. The working environment is pleasant and hospitable. A bank employee can expect to perform a wide variety of tasks and may participate in innovative applications of modern technology.

3. Banks are respected in the community. They are regarded as important establishments, and bank employees help people daily by providing money management and financial counseling. Because they are handling other people's money, bank employees at all levels must be trustworthy and reliable.

> **HUMAN RELATIONS TIP**
>
> Dependability inspires confidence.

# Organization Chart

So that you can better understand your role at Midtown Bank, the branch manager explains the functions of the bank and how each employee fits into the organization. In addition, the manager shares an organization chart with you (Figure I.1).

Midtown Bank tellers work closely with the bookkeeping, filing, customer service representatives, and proof departments. Bank employees are expected to be knowledgeable, efficient, understanding, and trustworthy. Customers need to be assured that their money will be handled safely by responsible employees.

You learn that "banker's hours" are longer than the open hours of the bank. Banks usually are open to the public five or six hours a day. Midtown Bank is open weekdays from 9 a.m. to 3 p.m. and Saturdays from 9 a.m. to 12 noon. Drive-thru windows are open from 8 a.m. to 6 p.m. Monday through Friday and from 8 a.m. to 12 noon on Saturday. Employees, however, must complete the processing of the day's transactions before the workday is over for them. Midtown Bank employees usually work a forty-hour week, with an occasional overtime period or weekend assignment.

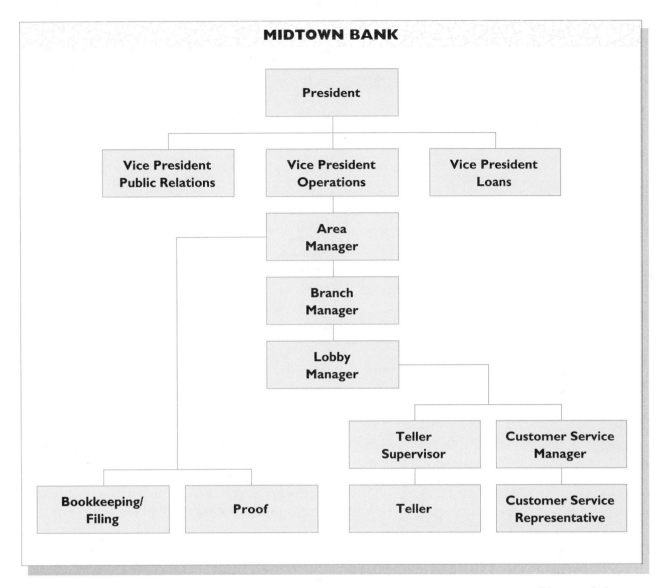

**MIDTOWN BANK**

President

Vice President Public Relations | Vice President Operations | Vice President Loans

Area Manager

Branch Manager

Lobby Manager

Teller Supervisor | Customer Service Manager

Bookkeeping/ Filing | Proof | Teller | Customer Service Representative

Figure I.1

*Organization*

*Chart for*

*Midtown Bank*

Take another look at the organization chart. Note that entry-level jobs consist of tellers, bookkeepers, file clerks, proof department employees, and customer service representatives. In your training at Midtown Bank, you will interact with all these employees. Once you are successful in your teller position, you may be able to perform in a higher level job. You may also wish to acquire more formal education to help you achieve your career goals.

## ■ Time Worked Record

All tellers at Midtown Bank are paid on an hourly basis and must keep a record of their working time so that their paychecks can be figured correctly. Midtown Bank uses a combination of automated and manual records to keep track of employee hours. To acquaint you with both methods of recording work time, you will be required to record your work time both on a **timecard** (shown in Figure I.2) and on the computer **time log**. You will enter your arriving and leaving times on the timecard each day. At the end of the simulation, you will figure the hours

## TIME WORKED RECORD

NAME _____

SOC. SEC. NO. _____

| DAY | DATE | TIME IN | TIME OUT | TOTAL HRS. |
|---|---|---|---|---|
| Monday | | | | |
| Tuesday | | | | |
| Wednesday | | | | |
| Thursday | | | | |
| Friday | | | | |
| | | | WEEKLY TOTAL | |

| DAY | DATE | TIME IN | TIME OUT | TOTAL HRS. |
|---|---|---|---|---|
| Monday | | | | |
| Tuesday | | | | |
| Wednesday | | | | |
| Thursday | | | | |
| Friday | | | | |
| | | | WEEKLY TOTAL | |

| DAY | DATE | TIME IN | TIME OUT | TOTAL HRS. |
|---|---|---|---|---|
| Monday | | | | |
| Tuesday | | | | |
| Wednesday | | | | |
| Thursday | | | | |
| Friday | | | | |
| | | | WEEKLY TOTAL | |

| DAY | DATE | TIME IN | TIME OUT | TOTAL HRS. |
|---|---|---|---|---|
| Monday | | | | |
| Tuesday | | | | |
| Wednesday | | | | |
| Thursday | | | | |
| Friday | | | | |
| | | | WEEKLY TOTAL | |

Employee's Signature _____

Supervisor's Signature _____

TOTAL HRS. THIS TIMECARD _____

**Figure I.2**

*Timecard*

you worked, sign the timecard, and submit the card to your supervisor. Each time you boot your computer, the Midtown Bank software will automatically record the time at which you begin work. When you exit the software, it will record your exit time. The payroll department will compute your earnings and prepare your paycheck from your computer time log. Deductions from your total pay—federal withholding taxes, social security taxes, and employee contributions to health care—will be computed by the payroll department.

The branch manager now introduces you to the teller supervisor who will be training you in your daily activities.

# ■ Work Assignments – Unit I

Congratulations! You are now a teller trainee in the Second Avenue Branch of Midtown Bank. As your supervisor, I'll help you learn our bank policies and teller procedures. Some of the things we'll discuss may seem unrelated to being a teller, but we believe our employees should know as much as possible about banking and should have a general knowledge of our policies. You'll learn these policies as part of your teller training.

After each day's training, you'll have Work Assignments to complete to see how well you've learned the procedures presented that day. Please complete each assignment as I give it to you so that you can concentrate on learning the procedure and will be able to complete it accurately. You will be paid at your regular rate of pay during this on-the-job training period. You may also be awarded bonus pay for exemplary work performance. Today, we'll discuss some of the procedures you will follow *every* day and introduce you to the Midtown Bank software.

## COMPLETING THE GENERAL WORKDAY PROCEDURES

Each day you will record your work hours on your timecard. You will record your work hours at Midtown Bank according to the following procedures:

1. Your timecard is included in the back of this *Employee Manual*. Do not remove this card. You will begin keeping your record today. Your timecard should show the actual class dates and times you use to complete simulation activities. Keep the card in your *Employee Manual* until you are ready to submit it to your supervisor at the end of the simulation.

2. Write your name and social security number at the top of the timecard.

3. Write today's actual date in the space opposite the appropriate day of the week.

4. Write the time your class begins in the space labeled "Time In."

5. When it is time to stop working, enter the exact time you stopped working on your assignment in the "Time Out" section of your timecard.

6. Complete the "Total Hours" section of the card each day by entering one of the following:

   Enter 1 if you work 50-60 minutes.
   Enter 3/4 if you work 35-49 minutes.
   Enter 1/2 if you work 20-34 minutes.
   Enter 1/4 if you work 5-19 minutes.
   Enter 0 if you are absent from class.

   **HUMAN RELATIONS TIP**

   Punctual employees are valued by their supervisors and by their coworkers.

   **Note:** If you are absent from work (class), enter the date you were absent, draw lines in the "Time In" and "Time Out" sections, and enter 0 in the "Total Hours" section for that day.

7. It is your responsibility to keep your timecard up to date. You will repeat Steps 3-6 each working (class) day.

8. At the end of each week, add the amounts in the "Total Hours" section for Monday through Friday and enter the total in the space labeled "Weekly Total."

9. When you have completed the simulation, you will total all your working hours, remove your timecard at the perforations, sign it, and submit it to your supervisor for verification.

## GETTING STARTED WITH THE MIDTOWN BANK SOFTWARE

Much of your work activity will be completed on the computer, which is on-line with the central office of Midtown Bank. You will be using the software on either an IBM®[1]PC (or compatible) or Macintosh®[2] computer.

Follow these steps to become acquainted with the Midtown Bank software:

1. Read Appendix A in this *Employee Manual* for a general overview of the Midtown Bank software.

2. Read and follow Appendix B in this *Employee Manual* to launch the Midtown Bank software. When the software is launched, your screen should look like the one shown in Figure I.3.

[1]IBM PC is a registered trademark of International Business Machines Corporation.
[2]Macintosh is a trademark of McIntosh Laboratory, Inc., and is used by Apple Computer, Inc., with its express permission.

**Figure I.3**

*Midtown Bank*

*Opening Screen*

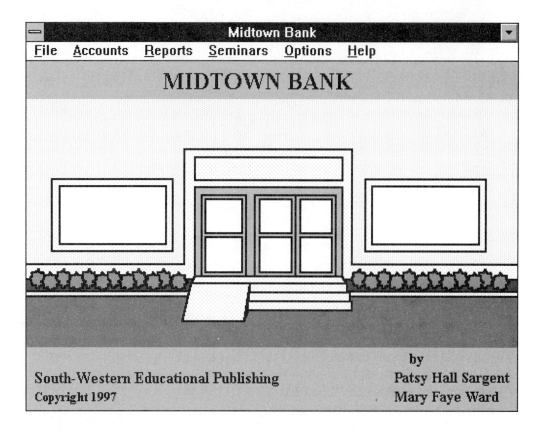

3. This is the first time you have used the Midtown Bank software, so you need to begin a new session. Pull down the File menu and choose the New command. When you are asked if you are a new student, click the Yes button.

4. Read the Midtown Bank Newsletter message. When you finish reading the message, click OK. The Employee Log (Figure I.4) will be displayed on your screen. This is the computer time log that will keep track of the time you spend using the Midtown Bank software.

5. You need to provide some information to the computer because this is the first time you have used the Employee Log. As you key the information required, you can use the delete and backspace keys to correct errors if necessary. Press TAB to move the cursor forward to the next field of the

**Figure I.4**

*Employee Log*

Employee Log; press SHIFT-TAB to move back to the previous field. You can also click the mouse to change fields.

- Key your first name, and then press TAB to move to the Last Name field.

- Key your last name. Press TAB to move to the Instructor's Name field.

- Click the arrow on the right side of the Instructor's Name field to display a list of instructors using the Midtown Bank software.

- Find your instructor in the list. Click your instructor's name to select it. Press TAB to move to the Password field.

- Choose a password. Choose your password carefully. It should be something that you can remember, but *not* something that other people can discover easily. (For example, you shouldn't use your first name or last name for your password.) You will need to use your password each time you use the Midtown Bank software, so make sure you use a word that has meaning to you. *Never tell anyone else what your password is, and do not write it down where others will see it.* (For example, do not write your password on a note and stick it on the side of the computer monitor.) You should treat your password as though it is a key to the bank's vault!

- Key your password in the Password field.

The rest of the Employee Log is filled out for you automatically as you use the Midtown Bank software.

- The Time In field shows the time you started using the software today.

- When you exit the software, the Time Out field will show the time you exited.

- The Time Worked field will show the total time you spent working with the Midtown Bank software.

- The Security Deficiencies field keeps track of security problems encountered as you use the software. For example, you will learn later in your training that you must lock the cash drawer each time you leave the teller window. If you leave the teller window and forget to lock the cash drawer, a message will appear in the Security Deficiencies box.

6. When you have completed the Employee Log, click OK to continue. If you chose a password that someone else is already using, you will be asked to enter a new password. Just key a new password in the Password field and click OK.

7. A message will appear telling you to remember your password and asking if you want to proceed. Click OK to continue.

8. The Midtown Bank lobby will appear on your screen.

9. Practice pulling down the menus on the Midtown Bank software. Take a look at each of the menus and commands available to you.

**HUMAN RELATIONS TIP**

Computer software helps bank tellers provide fast and accurate service to customers.

**10.** Pull down the File menu and choose the Exit/Quit command. Your time log will appear, showing how much time you spent working today. Click OK to exit the software. Click OK again when the message box appears asking you if you wish to exit. Finally, you will be asked if you would like to save your time worked record. Click Yes. **Note:** If another student will be using the software when you are finished, choose Close instead of Exit/Quit. This way, your data files will be closed, but the software will still be running for the next student. *You should always choose either Close or Exit/Quit when you are finished working for the day. Failure to do so will leave your files open for other students to use or alter.*

The next time you use the software, you will need to open your data files. To do this, just follow these steps:

- Launch the software.

- When the Midtown Bank opening screen appears, pull down the File menu and choose the Open command.

- Enter your password in the Password field. The rest of the information on the Employee Log will be completed for you automatically.

- Click OK. The Midtown Bank lobby will appear on your screen, and your data files will be ready for use.

Now that you are acquainted with Midtown Bank policies and have learned how to launch and navigate the software, complete the Unit Check Activity on pages 11-12 to check your understanding.

# Unit Check Activity                                    Unit I

**Instructions:** *Complete this activity using information from either the Employee Manual or the computer software. (Refer to Appendix A if necessary.) When you are finished, remove and submit your completed Unit Check to your instructor for evaluation.*

1. What is the name of your bank in this simulation?

   _____

2. What is the second command in the Accounts menu of this simulation?

   _____

3. Does the menu bar include a Calculator menu?

   _____

4. How many menu options are on the menu bar of the computer software? What are they?

   _____

   _____

   _____

5. What is the second command in the Options menu?

   _____

6. On the Midtown Bank organization chart, what is the next job above your position?

   _____

7. Do tellers work only the hours the bank is open to the public?

   _____

8. How many commands are in the File menu?

   _____

9. If you want information about a specific bank account, which command should you choose?

   _____

**10.** What is necessary for Midtown Bank tellers to access the computer system?

_____

_____

**11.** When the Midtown Bank lobby is displayed on your screen, what icons are included beneath the menu bar and Message box on the Midtown Bank software?

_____

_____

_____

_____

**12.** What are speed keys?

_____

_____

_____

_____

_____

**13.** Which icon should you click to find information about a customer's account?

_____

_____

**14.** Which icon should you click to unlock the cash drawer?

_____

_____

**15.** What is the difference between the Close command and the Exit/Quit command?

_____

_____

_____

_____

# CUSTOMER
# ACCOUNTS

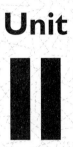
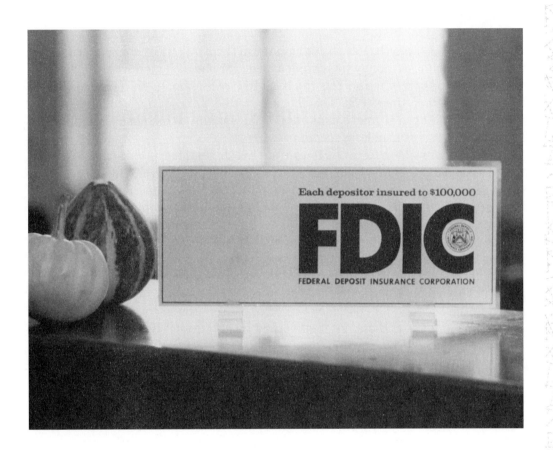

## *Objectives*

At the completion of Unit II, you will be able to:

- Understand how a bank handles money for its customers.
- Identify the different types of checking accounts and signature requirements.
- Use alphabetic, numeric, and microform filing.
- Use the Midtown Bank software to access customer information.

# Understanding Bank Accounts

In order to perform your teller duties well, you need to understand how a bank handles its customers' money. A customer must first open a **checking** or **savings account** at the bank. At this time, the customer signs a **signature (authorization) record** that gives the bank permission to withdraw money from the account on request. The signature on this record is the customer's *legal signature*. The bank gives each account a unique number that appears on all records of the account, including checks and deposit tickets. Then the customer puts money in the account. This is called depositing money in the bank. A **deposit** may consist of cash, checks, or other negotiable instruments. A **negotiable instrument** is a substitute for cash that can be used to exchange value instead of using cash. A **check** is a negotiable instrument because it represents cash and can be used for cash.

After the customer has deposited money in the bank, he or she may withdraw up to that amount of money by writing a check. A check signed with the legal signature of the owner authorizes the bank to pay the money to the person or business named on the check. The check is routed through the banking system until it reaches the customer's bank, where the amount of the check is subtracted from the customer's checking account.

Because banks look for ways to provide better service to their customers, they developed automatic teller machines. By using an **automatic teller machine (ATM)**, a customer can deposit money, withdraw money, or check a bank account balance. ATMs are found in convenient places such as shopping centers, airports, grocery stores, and in or near the bank itself. A customer would choose to use an ATM when it is in a more convenient place than the bank or when a transaction must be made after regular banking hours.

The bank periodically sends each of its customers a record of all account activity. This accounting record, called a **bank statement**, shows all deposits added to the account, all customer withdrawals from the account, any bank fees charged for service, and any interest earned on an interest-bearing account.

# Types of Checking Accounts

Midtown Bank offers several different types of checking accounts: individual, joint, business, and partnership. Signature requirements and signature (authorization) records differ for these various types of accounts. As a bank teller, you need to know the signature requirements for the different types of accounts. You don't want to give money to someone who is not authorized to receive it.

### INDIVIDUAL ACCOUNT

An individual account is owned by one person. Only the account owner can legally sign checks, using the same signature used on the bank's signature record.

Example:   Janet Welborne

*Janet Welborne*

## JOINT ACCOUNT

A joint or co-account is owned by two or more people. (A husband and wife are often joint owners of a checking account.) If names on the signature record are connected with the word *or*, only one account owner needs to sign checks written on the account. If the names on the signature record are connected with the word *and*, all co-owners' signatures are required on checks written against the account.

Example:    Justin *or* Barbara Sue Mulroney

*Justin Mulroney* _____ (Either)

*Barbara Sue Mulroney* _____ (Either)

Example:    Justin *and* Barbara Sue Mulroney

*Justin Mulroney* _____

*Barbara Sue Mulroney* _____ (Both)

## BUSINESS ACCOUNT

A business account is owned by a business firm. Individual officers of a business are authorized to sign checks written on the business account. Each officer authorized to sign company checks must complete and sign a signature record at the bank. The and/or rule that applies to joint accounts also applies to business accounts.

Example:    The Henderson Brothers Company, Inc.
Walter Henderson, President
or George Henderson, V.P. Finance

*Walter Henderson* _____ (Either)

## PARTNERSHIP ACCOUNT

A partnership account is owned by a partnership business firm. Individual partners are authorized to sign checks written on the partnership account. Each partner authorized to sign company checks must have a signature record on file at the bank. The and/or rule applies to partnership accounts, too.

Example:    Morgan, Lansing, and Washington, Attorneys-at-Law
James Morgan, Erica Lansing, or Matthew Washington

*Erica Lansing* _____ (Either)

# ■ Filing Systems

Before you look at some customer checks and deposits, you need to become familiar with Midtown Bank's filing systems. Filing is simply sorting and storing information in a particular order. Because customer account information needs to be reused from time to time—sometimes in a hurry—accurate sorting is very important. Filing in a bank is usually limited to **alphabetical** and **numerical computer sorting** and some **manual alphabetical filing** of hard copies of information. A **hard copy** is a paper record, as opposed to an electronic record on a computer.

The Second Avenue Branch of Midtown Bank maintains two customer files: the **Customer Information File** and the **Computer File**. First, we'll look at the kind of information in these files and why you need the information. Then, you'll learn some filing rules so you'll know how the information is filed and how to access it.

## CUSTOMER INFORMATION FILE

Midtown Bank's Customer Information File is a manual alphabetical file. This file is used primarily as a record of account information, including the customer's new account application, the signature record, copies of loans, and any other information that is necessary to identify the person or persons autho-

rized to use the account. These files are stored in fireproof cabinets so that business will not be interrupted in the event of a fire or other disaster. You need to be familiar with the files so you can access customer accounts to verify signatures or other account information in your daily job activities.

Midtown Bank files each original customer signature record at the branch where the account originated. These are hard copy files. An example of a signature record is shown in Figure II.1.

You can assume that signature records are on file at the branch of the bank where the account was opened. If a bank employee at another branch must compare a signature, a call to the branch holding the signature record to request a **fax** copy is necessary. A fax copy can be legally used as an original. This procedure requires a few minutes additional time but is required for questionable transactions and money withdrawals of $5,000 or more.

You can use the Midtown Bank software to "send" and "receive" faxes to verify signatures. After you have accessed the customer account information, just click the Send Fax button near the bottom of the dialog box to send or receive a fax.

**Figure II.1**

*Customer Signature*

*Record*

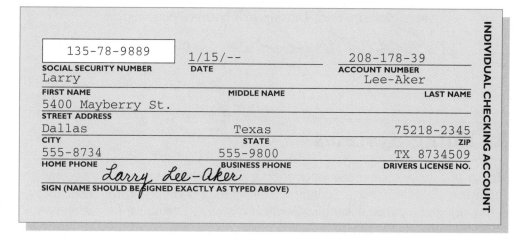

## COMPUTER FILE

Information about a customer that is necessary to maintain that customer's checking, savings, and loan accounts is stored in the computer and can be retrieved using either names or account numbers. The account information in the computer files originates from hard copy or completed forms (new account applications, deposits, withdrawals, and other transactions that are originated on paper). All checking and savings account transactions (deposits, withdrawals, bank fees, interest earned, and so forth) are entered into the computer for each account. Bank tellers may retrieve this account record in seconds, enter additional information or transactions, and make a copy of this updated information.

Customer accounts can be sorted both alphabetically by name and numerically by account number. You can access individual accounts by using account numbers. You can find an unknown account number by searching using the account name.

## MICROFORM FILE

In addition to the manual Customer Information File that has paper records and the Computer File that has electronic records, Midtown Bank also keeps a microform file. Checks, deposit tickets, and other documents relating to bank customers' accounts are photographed in **microform** daily at our main office location. Small pictures of the documents are indexed and located on a roll or sheet of film in such a way that one item can be relocated and duplicated quickly and inexpensively. This account information, as well as all account cash transactions, can also be accessed through the computer, but sometimes a hard copy is needed.

## ALPHABETIC FILING RULES

Alphabetical filing, of course, is based on the alphabet. Each signature record is filed according to the name of the account owner(s). An individual's name is divided into filing units. The last name is used for the first filing unit, called the *key unit*. Then the first name or initial is Unit 2, and the middle name or initial is Unit 3. Account names are keyed into a computerized list or database as separate filing units. The key unit is considered before any other unit for filing or sorting. The computer will sort the names automatically. Branch bank employees also maintain Customer Information Files by sorting and storing manually using the following guidelines. The chart following the rules shows examples of each of these alphabetic filing rules. **Note:** Filing units are written in all capital letters and no punctuation is used.

1. When comparing two names, the first different letter in a particular filing unit determines which name is first in alphabetical order. When a letter is being compared with no letter (nothing), then "nothing" comes before "something."

2. An article or particle in a name, such as D'Vincy, McDonald, VanAmber, O'Connell, or St. Charles, is part of the key unit.

3. Surnames that are compounded and separated with a hyphen are one filing unit.

4. Initials that are separate units go before all names that begin with that letter.

5. Titles and degrees are considered as filing units in alphabetic sequence. They are considered as the last unit.

6. Company names are indexed as they are written, except when *The* is the first word. If *The* is the first word, it is the last filing unit.

7. If a number is the key unit in a business name, the name is filed alphabetically before all names in words. Hyphenated words are treated as one filing unit.

8. Identical names are alphabetized according to the address: cities first, then states, then streets and numbers.

| RULE | ACCOUNT NAME | KEY UNIT | UNIT 2 | UNIT 3 |
|------|--------------|----------|--------|--------|
| 1. | Lee Harding | HARDING | LEE | |
| | Leesa M. Harding | HARDING | LEESA | M |
| | Lester W. Hardy | HARDY | LESTER | W |
| 2. | Sara Marie O'Connell | OCONNELL | SARA | MARIE |
| | St. Charles Computers | STCHARLES | COMPUTERS | |
| 3. | Erin Lee-Meadow | LEEMEADOW | ERIN | |
| 4. | A. Company, Inc. | A | COMPANY | INC |
| | Atlas Cleaners | ATLAS | CLEANERS | |
| 5. | Dr. Pat Jamison | JAMISON | PAT | DR |
| | Mrs. Phyllis Koenig | KOENIG | PHYLLIS | MRS |
| 6. | Joshua Long, Inc. | JOSHUA | LONG | INC |
| | Marchman and Sons | MARCHMAN | AND | SONS |
| | The Popcorn Man | POPCORN | MAN | THE |
| 7. | First-Class Realtors | FIRSTCLASS | REALTORS | |
| | Fourth Division | FOURTH | DIVISION | |
| 8. | Ziggy's, Atlanta | ZIGGYS | ATLANTA | |
| | Ziggy's, Dallas | ZIGGYS | DALLAS | |

## NUMERIC FILING RULES

*Figure II.2*

*Accounts Sorted*

*in Ascending*

*Numerical Order*

Although we do not maintain any manual numeric files at this branch, you will be accessing accounts by both number and name on the computer. Each account has a unique number assigned to it. This seven- to nine-digit number is printed on checks, deposit tickets, and other account documents to identify the correct bank account to be used for transactions.

If the account number is not known, click the Customer Accounts icon on the Midtown Bank software and key the last name of the account owner in the search field. This way the account number can be found. Accounts filed numerically are automatically sorted in **ascending order** by the computer. For example, 147-625-6 would be filed (or sorted) before 147-626-6. Figure II.2 shows customer account records arranged numerically by account numbers.

| | |
|---|---|
| Secure Storage | 338-461-8 |
| Eaton, Edward or Morma | 386-904-2 |
| Lucas, George | 386-951-2 |
| Lucas, George | 386-951-3 |
| Kirton, Henry | 387-968-4 |

# Using the Midtown Bank Software to Access Customer Information

You can access any account information, including all cash transactions, at your teller computer terminal. Before you do this, however, you need to understand about a special feature of the Midtown Bank software known as **bookmarking**. Please read the About Bookmarking box to learn about this feature of the software.

Follow these steps to learn how to access customer information and to practice using some of the features of the Midtown Bank software:

1. Launch the Midtown Bank software if you have not already done so.

2. Open your data file:

   ■ Pull down the File menu and choose the Open command.

   ■ Key your password in the Password field.

   ■ Click OK to open your file. The Midtown Bank lobby will appear on your screen.

3. Go to the Drive-thru window (just click the Drive-thru hot spot in the lobby), and then click the Customer Accounts icon. (Another way to access the customer accounts section of the software is to pull down the Accounts menu and choose the Customer command.) The Customer Account Access window shown in Figure II.3 will be displayed.

   The Customer Account Access window lets you scroll through the list box to find a customer. You can also search for customer account information by entering the customer's last name in the Search field at the bottom

## ABOUT BOOKMARKING

The Midtown Bank software is designed specifically for use with this simulation. The software expects you to access accounts in a certain way, enter specific transactions as they are presented in this *Employee Manual*, and so on.

Whenever you access an account, the Midtown Bank software moves a **bookmark** to record the fact that you accessed the account. Sometimes, access to a particular account causes something special to happen in the software. Maybe an instructional message will appear on the screen, or perhaps you will be praised for something you did particularly well.

In Units I-III, you will just be experimenting with the software to become more familiar with it. Therefore, the bookmark should not record the actions you take with the software. When the software records your actions, it is called **advancing the bookmarking**. To make sure the bookmarking is not advanced when you are just experimenting, you will be asked if you wish to advance the bookmarking each time you access a customer account. For now, click the No button when this dialog box appears. Beginning with Unit IV, you will want to advance the bookmarking so you can complete the Midtown Bank simulation.

Once you get to Unit IV, if you access an account by mistake, just click the No button when you are asked if you want to advance the bookmarking. This way, you can recover from your error without starting the entire simulation over again.

**Figure II.3**

*Customer Account*

*Access Window*

of the Customer Account Access window. This way, you can quickly find information even if the customer cannot remember his or her account number.

**Note:** By default, the customer account information is displayed in alphabetical order by customer last name. However, Midtown Bank employees also need to see information in numeric order by account number. The software provides an easy way for you to change the way the data are displayed: Just click the Setup button on the right side of the Customer Account Access window. In the Customer Account Setup dialog box, click the Numerical radio button, and then click OK. Now the information in the Customer Account Access window will be displayed in numeric order by account number. When data are displayed in numeric order, you can search for a specific account by entering the account number in the Search field.

So, here are the quick ways to find customer data:

- To find a customer by name, make sure the customer data are arranged in alphabetical order by customer name. Then key the customer's last name in the Search field or click on the scroll down button.

- To find a customer by account number, change the customer account information so it is arranged in numeric order by account number. Then key the account number in the Search field or click on the scroll down button.

For now, the account information should be in its default arrangement (alphabetical order according to last name). If it is not in that order, please change it before you continue.

**4.** To experiment with the Search feature, follow the steps below to find information about one of Midtown Bank's customers. Remember to click the No button whenever you are asked if you want to advance the bookmarking. Also, you might notice that special messages appear in the Message box near the top of the screen when you access certain accounts. For now, just ignore these messages. They will be important to you later in the simulation.

- Click in the Search field and key the following name:

**Petrosina**

As you key the name, the software jumps to Lella S. Petrosina's account and highlights her information in the Customer Account Access window.

- Click OK. Ms. Petrosina's information is displayed in the Customer Account window on your screen (Figure II.4).

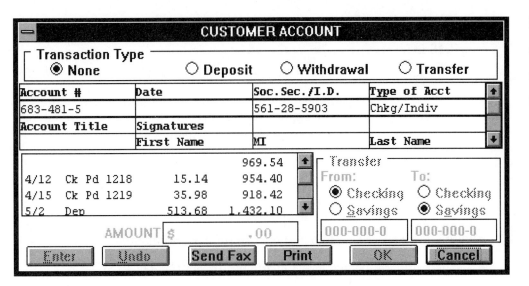

**Figure II.4**

*Account Information for Lella S. Petrosina*

The Transaction Type box at the top section of the Customer Account window lets you deposit, withdraw, or transfer money into or from an account. Notice that the next section of the Customer Account window provides information about Lella S. Petrosina, such as her social security number, the type of account, her address, and so on. You cannot change any of this information. Use the scroll down button to view all the information available.

A scroll box on the left side of the window details all of the transactions that have been processed in this account for the past 45 days. You can scroll through the box to see which checks have been paid, when deposits were made in the account, and so on. By scrolling to the last transaction, you can find the current balance in the account. When accessing an account, be sure to scroll to the bottom of the transactions list. Some accounts have important messages attached to the transactions list.

The Amount field is used to enter the dollar amount for deposits to and withdrawals from the account. It is not accessible right now because you haven't told the software that you want to record a transaction.

The Transfer box on the right side of the screen lets you transfer money from one of Ms. Petrosina's accounts to another. It is also not accessible right now; it will become active when you record a transaction.

You can print the information shown on the Customer Account screen by clicking the Print button.

You will learn more about using the Customer Account screen to process transactions later in your Midtown Bank training.

■ Click Cancel to return to the Drive-thru window.

■ Click No if you are asked if you would like to advance the bookmarking.

5. Click the Customer Accounts icon again to display the Customer Account Access window. This time, you will search for a customer by account number. Just follow these steps:

■ Click the Setup button to access the Customer Account Setup dialog box.

■ Click the Numerical radio button, and then click OK.

- Click in the Search field and key the following account number:

  **4510635**

  The Underhill Animal Clinic account is highlighted.

- Click OK to access the account information. Account information for the Underhill Animal Clinic will be displayed on your screen. Use the scroll down button to view all the information available.

- Click Cancel to return to the Drive-thru window.

- Click No if you are asked if you would like to advance the bookmarking.

6. If you are finished working for the day, exit the Midtown Bank software:

- Pull down the File menu and choose the Exit command.

- When your Employee Log appears on the screen, click OK.

- If you are asked if you wish to save your data, click No. **Note:** Exiting the simulation without saving your data can be dangerous! You should only do so when specifically instructed to do so in this *Employee Manual* or by your instructor. Right now you are just experimenting with the software, so you do not need to save your data. In most circumstances, however, you should save your data before you exit; failure to do so will cause your data to be lost.

Now that you know how to use the Midtown Bank software to find account information, you are ready to get to work. Your Work Assignment for today will provide practice in accessing accounts for information. You should have already recorded your beginning work time and day on your timecard. Follow the instructions for the Unit II Work Assignment to complete your work for the day.

**Name** _____     **Date** _____

---

## *Work Assignment*                                   *Unit II*

**Instructions:** *Use the Midtown Bank software to answer the following questions. In some cases you will only need to use the Search feature to determine the account number. For situations in which a customer has more than one account, or if you need to determine a bank balance or an address, you will need to actually look at the Customer Account screen. Use the Drive-thru window to access the Customer Account screen. Always remember to click No when you are asked if you would like to advance the bookmarking. When you have finished the Work Assignment, exit the Midtown Bank software but do not save your data.*

1. Find and write the account number for each of the following accounts.

| Account Name | Account Number |
| --- | --- |
| Phyllis A. or R. T. Lee (checking) | _____ |
| Anderson Brick Products | _____ |
| Linda J. Scott, M.D. (checking) | _____ |
| Shelly C. Wiemer (savings) | _____ |
| Dewey E. Scott | _____ |
| Alberto J. or Georgina L. Guerrero (savings) | _____ |

2. Find and write the account name for each of the following accounts.

| Account Number | Account Name |
| --- | --- |
| 683-945-6 | _____ |
| | _____ |
| 891-697-3 | _____ |
| | _____ |
| 684-932-5 | _____ |
| | _____ |
| 436-893-2 | _____ |
| | _____ |
| 861-593-2 | _____ |
| | _____ |

3. Write the address for each of the following accounts.

| Account Name | Account Address |
|---|---|
| Mauricio I. Alvarez (savings) | _____ |
| | _____ |
| Janis B. Wall | _____ |
| | _____ |
| Jorgenson Arts and Collectibles | _____ |
| | _____ |
| Trinity River Realtors | _____ |
| | _____ |

4. For each account listed below, indicate whether the account is a checking or a savings account, provide the account type (joint, individual, and so on), and indicate the signatures required for the account. Write your answers in the blanks provided.

| Account Number | Checking/ Savings | Type of Account | Signatures Required |
|---|---|---|---|
| 487-643-6 | _____ | _____ | _____ |
| 581-496-1 | _____ | _____ | _____ |
| 386-951-3 | _____ | _____ | _____ |
| 596-431-2 | _____ | _____ | _____ |
| 493-682-5 | _____ | _____ | _____ |

5. Write the current balance of each of these accounts.

| Account Number | Current Balance |
|---|---|
| 893-462-1 | _____ |
| 684-938-1 | _____ |
| 483-461-5 | _____ |
| 386-904-2 | _____ |
| 862-543-1 | _____ |

Remove the Work Assignment and submit it to your instructor for evaluation.

## Unit Check Activity                                      Unit II

**Instructions:** *Complete this activity using the information in Unit II or by accessing customer accounts on the computer while in the Drive-thru window. (When you access accounts on the computer, remember to click No when you are asked if you want to advance the bookmarking.) Circle the correct answer, fill in the blank, or write a short answer. When you are finished, remove and submit your completed Unit Check to your instructor for evaluation.*

**1.** By default, items in the Customer Account Access window are arranged according to (numeric, alphabetic) filing rules.

**2.** When arranged numerically, account records in the Customer Account Access window are filed numerically in (descending, ascending) order.

**3.** A checking account that may be used by more than one person is called a(n) (individual, joint) account.

**4.** Using alphabetic filing rules, which comes first, McDowell or Walls?

_____

**5.** If a customer signature record is filed at another bank branch location, the teller may access a copy by

_____

**6.** What is the account name of account No. 864-349-2?

_____

**7.** What is the account number of Henry R. Kirton's account?

_____

**8.** What is the current balance of account No. 469-583-2?

_____

**9.** What is the amount of the last deposit for account No. 586-391-2?

_____

**10.** What is the current address of the checking account owned by Earl L. and Amy S. Eddings?

_____

**11.** Surnames that are compounded and separated with a hyphen are (one, two) filing unit(s).

**12.** If the names on the signature record of a bank account are "John and Gail Rogers," checks should be signed by (both, either) party(ies).

**13.** When alphabetizing names, if a letter is being compared with no letter, then (something, nothing) comes first.

**14.** Write the following name in correct filing order:

James R. O'Brien

Key Unit _____

Unit 2 _____

Unit 3 _____

**15.** A teller may access a specific customer account on the computer by using the account (number, type).

# CHECKS AND DEPOSITS

## *Objectives*

At the completion of Unit III, you will be able to:

- Identify the parts and functions of a check.
- Identify the parts and functions of a deposit ticket.
- Explain the types and purposes of check endorsements.
- Use a numeric keypad by touch.

# Handling Checks

When you finish your training and begin working at your teller window, you will be handling all sorts of checks every day. You need to know all about checks so you can perform your duties as a teller efficiently and accurately. A check is a paper instrument that represents money. When a person writes and signs a check, it indicates that:

1. The person has a checking account with the financial institution.

2. The person has sufficient funds to pay the check.

3. The person is authorized to sign the check.

Checks are called negotiable instruments because they can be used as cash. Other negotiable instruments that are handled the same way as checks are money orders, traveler's checks, and cashier's checks. As shown in Figure III.1, all checks involve three parties:

1. **Drawer.** The party who requests that payment be made.

2. **Drawee.** The party (always a financial institution) who pays the money to the payee.

3. **Payee.** The party who receives the money.

**Figure III.1**

*An Illustration of a*

*Check*

Checks should be written carefully, legibly, and accurately, whether a pen, typewriter, stamp, or checkwriting machine is used. The following guidelines explain Midtown Bank's policies for accepting checks. Refer to the sample check shown in Figure III.2 as you read.

1. **Date.** The current date is normally used. Occasionally, however, the drawer may **postdate** a check (use a date later than the current date). *Midtown Bank does not accept postdated checks before the date that appears on the check.* A check with no date can be accepted whenever it is presented for payment.

2. **Payee.** A check can be paid to a payee party as order paper or bearer paper. **Order paper** means that a check is written *Pay to the order of* a particular party, such as:

   - A person or persons—LeAnn Walls
   - A company—Quality Paper Company
   - A position—President, Quality Paper Company
   - A fund—United Way

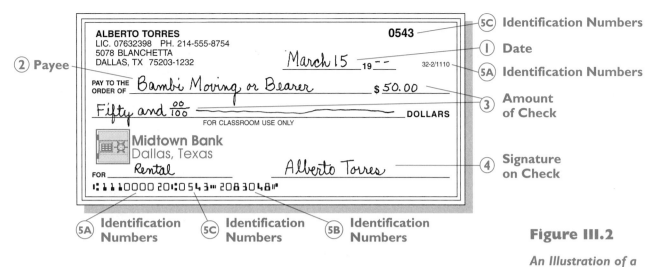

Figure III.2

*An Illustration of a*

*Check*

The check with *Bambi Moving* as the payee (Figure III.1) is an example of order paper.

**Bearer paper** is written *Pay to the order of* one of the following:

- Cash

- Bearer

- Named payee (person, company name, position, and so on) *or bearer*—
  Vicki Stanley or Bearer

The check illustrated in Figure III.2 showing *Bambi Moving or Bearer* as the payee is an example of bearer paper.

**Note:** Legally, order paper must be endorsed by the named payee to be cashed or transferred for value. Bearer paper may be cashed or transferred by anyone who holds the check. An explanation of endorsements appears later in this unit.

3. **Amount of Check.** The amount of a check must be a definite sum of money. As a bank employee, you should determine whether or not the amount has been altered in any way and whether the amount in words is the same as the amount in numbers. When the word and number amounts are not the same, the amount in words is the legal amount of the check.

4. **Signature on Check.** A check must be signed by the drawer with the exact signature(s) shown on the account signature record. Signature requirements can be verified by accessing the customer account. A signature may be faxed from one location to another in minutes if a signature comparison is needed.

5. **Identification Numbers.** Numbers and symbols printed on the face of a check identify both the customer's account and the customer's bank:

- The numbers labeled 5A identify the individual bank, its city or state, and the Federal Reserve routing for the bank. These numbers are specifically identified for the partial check shown in Figure III.3.

- The numbers labeled 5B identify the customer's account.

- The number labeled 5C corresponds to the account owner's check number printed in the upper right corner of the check.

The check shown in Figure III.2 is called a *personalized check* because the customer's name, address, and any other identification information is preprinted in the upper left corner of the check. All the numbers and symbols printed at the bottom of the check are in magnetic ink to make it possible for each check

Figure III.3

*Check Identifica-*

*tion Numbers*

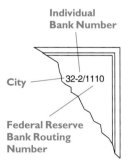

paid to be listed electronically by number in the customer's account record. When checks reach the bank's proof department, the dollar amount will be encoded in magnetic ink on the bottom right margin for further processing.

In most instances, checks presented to you will be authentic in every way. However, you must be alert at all times to checks that are not genuine in some way, that is, those that have been forged or altered. Some checkpoints for validity are the following:

1. All checks should be perforated on at least one side.

2. All checks must have bank routing numbers and the customer account number on the bottom margin.

3. There should not be any obvious changes in the writing of the check (changes in the color of ink, water damage, erasures, and so on).

# Other Negotiable Instruments

**Figure III.4**

*Money Order*

The negotiable instruments in the following illustrations are very similar to a check. As you examine them, you will notice that each has a *drawer*, a *drawee*, and a *payee*. These negotiable instruments are handled the same way as you handle checks.

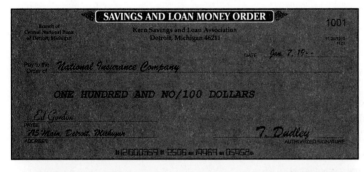

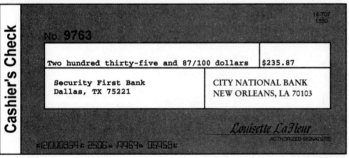

1. **Money Order.** A money order (shown in Figure III.4) is a check drawn on an agency's or bank's own account by an authorized officer of that agency or bank.

2. **Cashier's Check.** A check drawn on a bank by one of its own officers is known as a cashier's check (Figure III.5).

3. **Traveler's Check.** A traveler's check (shown in Figure III.6) is a check that is insured by some agency or bank for use by the purchaser while traveling away from home.

**Figure III.5**

*Cashier's Check*

**Figure III.6**

*Traveler's Check*

# Handling Deposits

In addition to handling checks, you will be accepting deposits—additions to customers' bank accounts—at your teller window. Deposits consist of a **deposit ticket** accompanied by money. The money can be in the form of cash, negotiable instruments, or both. Deposit tickets, like checks, are frequently personalized.

All deposit tickets contain essentially the same information, though they may vary in size and in the arrangement of the information. The following information is needed by the bank to process a deposit to a customer's account. Refer to the sample deposit ticket shown in Figure III.7 as you read.

1. **Account Name and Address and Other Identification.** This information is usually preprinted on the deposit ticket.

2. **Date of Deposit.**

3. **Coins and Currency.** The coins and currency should be listed separately.

4. **Checks/Negotiable Instruments.** The checks and other negotiable instruments should be listed separately according to one of the following:
   - Name of drawer
   - Individualized check number
   - Bank number
   - Location (city and state) of the drawee bank

   For simplicity, all checks should be listed using the same format. A business depositing many checks often uses an adding tape to show only the total of the checks.

5. **Total.** All coins, currency, and checks and other negotiable instruments are added to provide the total amount.

6. **Less Cash Received.** If a depositor wishes to subtract an amount from the deposit total and receive that amount in cash, he or she enters that amount here.

7. **Signature.** If a customer receives cash from the deposit, a signature is required to authorize subtracting cash received from the total deposit amount.

8. **Total of Deposit.** This is the amount after any cash received by the customer is subtracted. It is the amount that will be added to the customer's account.

9. **Identification Numbers.** The identification numbers are the same as those preprinted on personalized checks (see Figure III.2), except deposit tickets are not numbered consecutively. This information may also be handwritten.

**Figure III.7**

*Deposit Ticket*

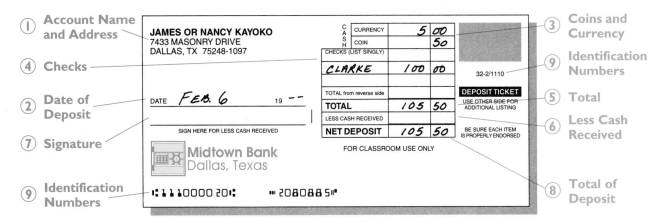

# Endorsements

**Figure III.8**

*Proper Endorse-*

*ment Placement*

As a teller, you must carefully examine all checks presented for deposit. After examining the face of a check, turn it over to see that proper endorsement has been made. The **endorsement** is the signature that the payee(s) writes on the back of the check when the check is presented for the cash it represents. The payee must write the name as it appears on the face of the check. Figure III.8 shows the correct placement of an endorsement as designated by the U.S. Congress in 1988.

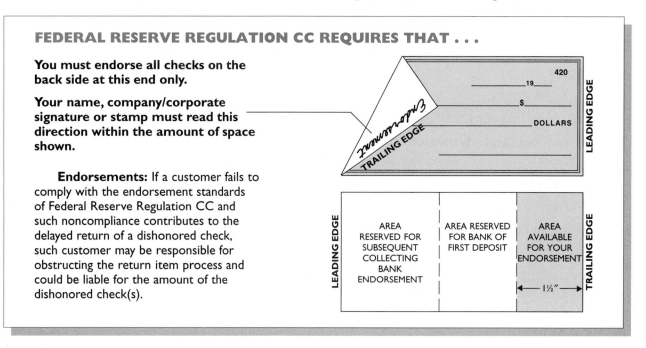

**FEDERAL RESERVE REGULATION CC REQUIRES THAT . . .**

**You must endorse all checks on the back side at this end only.**

**Your name, company/corporate signature or stamp must read this direction within the amount of space shown.**

**Endorsements:** If a customer fails to comply with the endorsement standards of Federal Reserve Regulation CC and such noncompliance contributes to the delayed return of a dishonored check, such customer may be responsible for obstructing the return item process and could be liable for the amount of the dishonored check(s).

**Figure III.9**

*Blank Endorsement*

One of your responsibilities as a teller will be to recognize the different types of endorsements described and illustrated in the following list.

1. **Blank Endorsement.** A blank endorsement is only a signature. It makes bearer paper of the check; that is, anyone can transfer it for money after the blank endorsement is written. An example of a blank endorsement is shown in Figure III.9.

2. **Restrictive Endorsement.** Checks endorsed with a restrictive endorsement cannot be used for any reason other than the stated restriction. Most deposited checks are endorsed with the restriction "For deposit only." (See Figure III.10.)

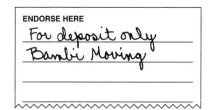

**Figure III.10**

*Restrictive Endorsements*

3. **Special or Full Endorsement.** This endorsement makes order paper of the check and includes the name of a new payee, stating exactly to whom the check is to be transferred. The party named in the endorsement must then be the party who cashes or transfers the check. This makes the check a three-party check. A **three-party check** is one that has a drawer, a payee, and an endorsee that are all different (Figure III.11). *Our tellers do not cash three-party checks*

MISS ALICE HALL                                         0420
LIC. 08593020   PH. 214-555-5060
115 PALMERSTON
DALLAS, TX  75211-1197                    March 15 19--        32-2/1110
                          ②

PAY TO THE
ORDER OF   Bambi Moving                        $50⁰⁰

   Fifty and ⁰⁰/100 ~~~~~~~~~~~~~~~ DOLLARS
              FOR CLASSROOM USE ONLY

      Midtown Bank
      Dallas, Texas                              ①
FOR      Rental              Miss Alice Hall

⑈1110000 20⑈04 20⑈ 7 15 240 3⑈

---

ENDORSE HERE

Bambi Moving
Pay to Jim Coons  ③
Jim Coons

**Figure III.11**

*Three-party Check*

*unless the payee or the drawer of the check is one of Midtown Bank's customers.* Proper identification should be carefully noted whenever three-party checks are presented at the teller window.

Endorsements may be handwritten, typed, or stamped. Businesses usually use an endorsement stamp because it is faster and easier than using handwriting. If the payee of a check includes two or more parties connected with the word *and*, all parties must endorse the check. If the payee names two or more parties connected with the word *or*, then only one party is required to endorse the check.

# ■ Using the Numeric Keypad

Much of your work in handling money will be completed with the numeric keypad on the computer. All new employees must learn the touch method for numeric keypad operation; this helps ensure fast, accurate operation. Your computer has a numeric keypad on the right side of the keyboard. Make sure the Num Lock light on your computer is on. Follow the instructions provided to practice using the Midtown Bank software numeric keypad.

**HUMAN RELATIONS TIP**

By being fast and accurate when using the numeric keypad, bank tellers can provide better service to their customers.

## USING THE TOUCH METHOD

Your forearm should be parallel to the right edge of the computer keyboard. Your wrist should be flat—neither held up nor resting on the keyboard. Operate the keys with your right hand; keep your left hand free to follow figures or handle papers.

Curve your fingers over the **home keys**, the 4, 5, and 6 keys. You should be able to reach the keys above and below the home keys easily. (Some keypads have a bump on the 5 key to indicate the home row.) Operate the 4, 7, and 1 keys with your index finger. Operate the 5, 8, and 2 keys with your middle finger; and operate the 6, 9, and 3 keys with your ring finger. Operate the plus (+), minus (–), and enter keys, usually on the right of the keypad, with your little finger. Operate the divide (/) and multiply (*) keys with the appropriate "in-line" fingers. Operate the 0 and/or 00 keys with your thumb. Your computer may be configured a little differently, and you may need to adjust the fingering. Ask your supervisor for help if needed.

Because using two decimal places is most appropriate when listing dollars and cents amounts, the Midtown Bank software keypad will automatically set figures for two decimals. This means that you do not need to press the decimal key. It also means that you may need to add zeros to some numbers. For example, to enter an amount of $4.00, you need to key **400** (not just **4**).

Follow these steps to practice using the numeric keypad. **Note:** You will not open your data file just yet. This practice is "off the clock," which means the time you spend on this activity will not be added to your electronic time log.

1. Launch the Midtown Bank software.

2. Pull down the Options menu and choose the Keypad command. The Keypad window shown in Figure III.12 will appear on your screen.

3. Click the Clear button to clear the numeric keypad. **Note:** Although the keypad is clear when you first access the software, it is a good idea to get in the habit of clicking the Clear button whenever you begin entering a new set of numbers. This way, you can be sure that you are starting with a clean slate.

4. To key 4.44:
   - Curve your fingers over the home keys.
   - Tap the keys one at a time; key **444** with your index finger. Notice that the number is entered with two decimal places, so your entry looks like this: 4.44.

5. Press the plus (+) key to *register* 4.44 into the keypad. Note that if you are subtracting a number, you should press the minus (–) key instead of the plus (+) key to register the number. Do *not* use ENTER to register the number. Pressing ENTER tells the software that you are finished entering the list.

6. Key **555** with your middle finger. Register.

7. Key **666** with your ring finger. Register.

8. Press ENTER to total the numbers. **Note:** Once you press ENTER, you cannot make any corrections or changes to your number list. Make sure you have carefully checked your list before you press ENTER.

9. Click the Clear button to clear the numeric keypad. This allows you to enter a new list of numbers. (You can also clear the keypad by pressing ENTER a second time.)

10. Key the following lists of numbers to practice using the numeric keypad:

| 1.11 | 4.44 | 7.77 | 1.76 |
|---|---|---|---|
| 2.22 | 5.55 | 8.88 | 3.47 |
| 3.33 | 4.44 | 9.99 | 8.92 |
| 2.22 | 5.55 | 7.77 | 5.32 |
| 3.33 | 6.66 | 8.88 | 7.13 |
| 12.21 | 26.64 | 43.29 | 26.60 |

Remember, you don't need to key the total of the numbers. Just press ENTER after all of the numbers in the list have been keyed, and the total will be displayed automatically. After each list has been totaled, you need to clear the keypad before you begin keying the next list.

Also remember that to subtract, enter the amount to be subtracted, then register the entry with the minus (–) key instead of the plus (+) key.

To multiply, key the number to be multiplied and press the plus (+) key to register. Then key the multiplier and press the times (*) key to register. Now press ENTER, or the equals (=) key if your keypad has one. The Keypad window will show the product. Remember that the keypad automatically adds a decimal so whole numbers need to be keyed followed by two zeros.

KEY PAD

.00|

Clear   Cancel

**Figure III.12**

*Keypad Window*

Example:    2 × 5 = 10    Key **200+**.    Keypad will show 2.00
                          Key **500\***.    Keypad will show 5.00
                          Press ENTER.    Keypad will show 10.00

If you press the wrong key and have not yet registered the amount into the keypad, remove the incorrect number by using the arrow keys to position the cursor to the left of the incorrect number and then pressing the delete key. Locate the arrow and delete keys on your computer and determine which finger will be the most convenient for you to use for the touch method.

If you realize that you have just keyed a wrong amount, immediately arrow over and press the delete key until you have deleted the wrong amount. Make sure to do this *before* you register the number. If you do not notice the wrong amount until after other numbers have been registered, enter the wrong number again and press the minus (–) key (or the plus (+) key if the wrong amount was originally registered with the minus (–) key). You will then be ready to enter the correct amount.

**11.** When you are finished working, pull down the File menu and choose the Exit command.

## GETTING STARTED WITH THE KEYPAD WORKSHOP

To help you learn how to operate the numeric keypad proficiently, the Midtown Bank software includes a built-in Keypad Workshop. By working through the Keypad Workshop, you can earn extra pay. The more accurate you are with the numeric keypad, the more likely you are to earn a bonus. Therefore, you should always key numbers as accurately as possible.

To use the Keypad Workshop, follow these steps:

**1.** Launch the Midtown Bank software.

**2.** Open your data file.

**3.** Pull down the Seminars menu and choose the Keypad Workshop command. The Keypad Workshop window shown in Figure III.13 will be displayed on your screen.

Notice the scroll bar on the right side of the window. You can use the scroll bar to scroll to the beginning of a long list of data. The buttons at the bottom of the Keypad Workshop window are used as follows:

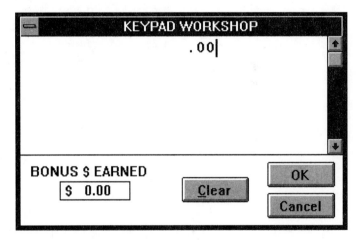

**Figure III.13**

*Keypad Workshop*

*Window*

■ **OK.** Use this button to indicate that you are finished entering data for the time being, *even if you haven't completed the entire workshop.* If you get halfway through a list of numbers and need to quit, click the OK button. The software will return to the Midtown Bank lobby. Your data will not be saved, but you can pick up with this column of data next time you use the Keypad Workshop, and you will still have an opportunity to earn a bonus for this column. You should also click the OK button when you are finished entering data and *you have completed the workshop.*

■ **Clear.** Use this button to erase everything in the Keypad Workshop window. The cursor will be positioned at the top of the window for you to begin entering more data. When you click Clear, all data displayed in the Keypad

Workshop window are lost. Therefore, you should use this button only when you need to start a column of numbers over from the beginning.

- **Cancel.** Use this button to cancel *all* work completed in the Keypad Workshop during this session. The data displayed in the Keypad Workshop window will be erased and you will lose any bonus you have earned for this session. The Keypad Workshop window will be closed, and the software will return to the Midtown Bank lobby. You should use this button only if you want to start the workshop over from the beginning.

Finally, note the **Bonus box** at the left side of the Keypad Workshop window. This box shows the bonus you have earned. Hard work pays off at Midtown Bank!

4. Practice adding the following lists. Keep your eyes on the copy as you work and use the touch method. *If you do not key the correct numbers, the total will not print. If a total prints, you have keyed the list correctly.* Do not go to the next list until you have achieved a correct answer.

| 1. | 2. | 3. | 4. | 5. |
|---|---|---|---|---|
| 4.56 | 5.85 | 6.96 | 7.48 | 4.14 |
| 6.54 | 5.86 | 6.99 | 5.86 | 4.12 |
| 4.56 | 5.84 | 6.95 | 6.97 | 1.23 |
| 5.46 | 8.45 | 5.59 | 8.67 | 2.41 |
| 5.46 | 5.88 | 9.69 | 6.58 | 4.41 |
| 4.74 | 5.86 | 6.96 | 8.56 | 1.45 |
| 4.75 | 5.85 | 9.64 | 5.89 | 4.44 |
| 4.77 | 8.85 | 6.94 | 6.48 | 1.41 |
| 5.47 | 8.56 | 4.66 | 4.87 | 4.15 |

| 6. | 7. | 8. | 9. | 10. | 11. |
|---|---|---|---|---|---|
| 5.25 | 3.63 | 5.28 | 4.04 | 6.09 | 1.70 |
| 5.23 | 6.36 | 3.25 | 6.06 | 6.30 | 3.90 |
| 2.34 | 3.65 | 8.56 | 9.09 | 4.00 | 2.00 |
| 5.26 | 3.64 | 7.68 | 5.80 | 6.00 | 7.01 |
| 2.52 | 6.45 | 9.53 | 4.20 | 4.01 | 9.03 |
| 5.25 | 3.63 | 5.63 | 3.00 | 2.20 | 8.70 |
| 5.24 | 3.66 | 1.25 | 1.00 | 2.02 | 9.00 |
| 5.26 | 6.34 | 6.91 | 1.50 | 3.07 | 1.70 |
| 5.45 | 4.66 | 3.69 | 5.00 | 10.00 | 30.00 |

5. After you have correctly entered all 11 columns of numbers and clicked OK, your Keypad Workshop answers are displayed on the screen. Click the Print button near the bottom of the dialog box. Click OK in the Print dialog box to print your answers. Sign the answer sheet and give it to your supervisor for evaluation.

6. Close the Keypad Workshop window. Pull down the File menu and choose the Save command.

7. Exit the Midtown Bank software:

- Pull down the File menu and choose the Close command.
- When your Employee Log is displayed on the screen, click OK.
- When you are asked if you want to close the scenario, click OK.

As a teller, you should work quickly and accurately to accommodate the daily customer load. If you think you need to complete the Keypad Workshop again, do so now. When you are ready to use the numeric keypad to complete your work activities for the day, continue to the Unit III Work Assignment.

# Work Assignment                                    *Unit III*

**Instructions:** *Continue your time worked record. You will be examining checks and deposit tickets that were prepared for your practice and will be using the numeric keypad in the Midtown Bank software. Be sure to save your file and exit the software properly when you have finished the Work Assignment.*

1. Remove the checks labeled III-1 through III-18 from the back of this *Employee Manual* and separate them at the perforations. Examine each check for the following items. Circle and correct any errors or omissions you find on the checks.

   ■ The check should be signed using the correct party's signature. If you are in doubt, access the customer's account while in the Drive-thru window, but *do not advance the bookmarking*. If you need to verify an actual signature, use the fax. To use the fax, just access the customer account and choose the Send Fax button.

   ■ The amount written in words should be the same as the amount written in numbers.

   ■ The check should not be dated later than today's date (postdated). Use May 17 as today's date.

   ■ The check should be endorsed properly.

2. Launch the Midtown Bank software if you have not already done so. Click the Keypad icon to activate the numeric keypad.

3. Using the touch method, enter the correct amount of each check. Use your left hand to turn over each check as you enter the amount to add.

4. Total the checks.

5. Add and total the checks again. If you do not get the same total, then you have made an error. Re-add until you get the same total twice. When you are satisfied with your result, write the total here:

   _____

6. Manually, sort these same eighteen checks into numerical filing order using account numbers. List the account numbers in correct numerical order at the right. (List the first nine checks in the left-hand column and the last nine checks in the right-hand column.)

**7.** Remove the deposit tickets labeled III-19 through III-30 from the back of this *Employee Manual* and separate them at the perforations. Use the numeric keypad to verify the addition and subtraction on each deposit ticket. If you find an error, circle and correct the error on the deposit ticket.

**8.** Manually sort the twelve deposit tickets into alphabetic order using account names. If you need help, refer to the alphabetic filing rules in Unit II. List the deposit tickets in correct alphabetical order here.

_____

_____

_____

_____

_____

_____

_____

_____

_____

Remove the Work Assignment, the checks, and the deposit tickets and submit them to your instructor for evaluation.

# Unit Check Activity                                    Unit III

**Instructions:** *For each of the following statements, write a T if the statement is true or an F if the statement is false. When you are finished, remove and submit your completed Unit Check to your instructor for evaluation.*

_____  1. All checks being deposited should have a proper endorsement on the back.

_____  2. All coins and currency are listed together as one amount when entered on a deposit ticket.

_____  3. If the amount of a check in figures differs from the amount in words, the amount in figures is correct.

_____  4. Negotiable instruments, such as traveler's checks and money orders, are treated as checks on deposit tickets.

_____  5. The payee of a check is the party to whom the check is payable.

_____  6. A check endorsed "Pay to the order of Jane Smith" has a blank endorsement.

_____  7. A check that has a date later than today's date is called a predated check.

_____  8. A check written payable to John Jackson is order paper.

_____  9. A check written payable to Cash is bearer paper.

_____  10. The endorsement is the signature of the payee on the back of the check.

_____  11. If a customer making a deposit wishes to receive some cash, he or she must endorse the back of the deposit ticket.

_____  12. The drawee of a check is the party who requests that payment be made.

_____  13. The 6 key on a numeric keypad may have a bump on it to help the operator with finger placement.

_____  14. The home keys on a computer keypad are the 7, 8, and 9 keys.

_____  15. The index finger operates the 1, 4, and 7 keys on a computer keypad.

# CUSTOMER RELATIONS AND CASH HANDLING

## Unit

# IV

## Objectives

At the completion of Unit IV, you will be able to:

- Answer questions about customers' accounts.

- Provide customers with information about bank services.

- Understand the procedure for counting and packaging money.

- Recognize the difference between real and counterfeit currency.

- Simulate receiving and disbursing money.

- Verify the accuracy of your money handling activities.

# Customer Relations and Bank Services

As a teller, you are a public relations representative of Midtown Bank. Customers see tellers more than any other bank employees because tellers perform many important functions for the bank and its customers. Your most obvious duties are receiving customers' deposits and cashing checks at your teller window. However, tellers also answer customers' questions or direct them to the appropriate bank employee.

All bank customers should be treated with respect and courtesy. Bank customers want their financial transactions to be handled efficiently by employees who are both knowledgeable about bank functions and happy to perform bank services. We'll start your training today by considering some of Midtown Bank's services.

## CUSTOMER ACCOUNT INFORMATION REQUESTS

Customers frequently ask tellers for assistance or for information about their accounts. When a customer requests account information, assist with the request as soon as possible, asking your supervisor for help if necessary. Write the customer's name, account number (if known), account type, and the requested information on a form like the one shown in Figure IV.1. This form serves as a written memo for the convenience of the customer.

**Figure IV.1**

*Request for Customer Information Form*

**REQUEST FOR CUSTOMER INFORMATION**

Name

Acct. No.

Acct. Type

Last Deposit

Comments

All customer information is privileged, which means that a bank employee can reveal a customer's account information only to the account owner. Financial status is a personal matter, and Midtown Bank has very strict rules for identifying persons asking for information. You should use the following procedure when a customer requests information about a bank account:

1. Ask for the name and account number of the person requesting the information.

2. Ask for the date and the amount of the last deposit made to verify the customer's identity. Check the customer's deposit information by accessing the customer's account on the Midtown Bank software. (You can access an account by using the Customer command in the Accounts menu.)

3. If you cannot find a record of the deposit, you may wish to ask for a driver's license number for additional identification. If you still cannot find a matching record, do *not* give any account information to the person.

4. If you can confirm the customer's deposit, write the customer's requested information on the Request for Customer Information Form and give the form to the customer.

Our tellers are not responsible for telephone requests because our customer service representatives handle them. However, if you should answer the telephone, answer with "Midtown Bank, teller window." Be cordial and businesslike. You should also mention to customers who telephone for account information that they may call our 800 number, where account information is available by voice mail 24 hours a day.

A frequently asked question at the teller window is, "What is the balance of my checking account?" First, you should verify the customer's identity by the procedure above—the customer's account number and the amount of the last deposit in the account. Then find the account balance by accessing the account on the Midtown Bank software. Other account information, such as the amount of a certain check or whether a particular check has been paid, is also available in the Customer Account window. As you learned in Unit II, you can trace checking and savings account transactions for the past 45 days in the Customer Account window of the Midtown Bank software.

## CUSTOMER ASSISTANCE AND COUNSELING

A customer may need a bank employee's assistance in verifying an account balance because several transactions in his or her file may need to be reviewed. If you are very busy or if the request is extensive, you may refer the customer to a customer service representative.

Refrain from telling a bank customer anything about his or her account while away from bank records. The information could be incorrect, causing embarrassment for Midtown Bank or individual employees.

## BANK SERVICES INFORMATION

As a Midtown Bank teller, you might be asked questions such as these: "I need to get a bank loan. Can you help me?" "I'm having a meeting of my book club, and I understand you have a room I can use. Tell me about it. Is it available?" "I'd like to open a checking account. What do I do?" You should be as helpful as possible when customers ask about bank services. If you are not equipped to help them at the teller window, you should direct them to the appropriate bank employee. The following services are provided by the bank employee indicated:

1. **Checking and Savings Accounts.** Customer service representatives open all new accounts, accept check orders, and provide other similar services to account owners. Refer a customer to this area by simply clicking on the customer service representative hot spot in the Midtown Bank software.

2. **Loans.** If a customer asks you about a loan, refer the customer to the loan officer. Tellers are not authorized to make loans, so be friendly and helpful but do not make a commitment that cannot be met. Direct customers who want to make loan payments to the loan teller window. **Note:** You do not need to do anything in the Midtown Bank software to refer a customer to the loan officer or the loan teller window. Just be aware that you should not try to handle these types of transactions on your own.

3. **Miscellaneous Services.**

- **Safe Deposit Boxes.** Refer the customer to a customer service representative.

- **Negotiable Instruments.** Customers must purchase money orders, cashier's checks, and traveler's checks at the customer service representative desk. If a customer requests one of these instruments, just click the customer service representative hot spot in the Midtown Bank software. Although you will not actually see the negotiable instrument, you can be confident the customer will receive prompt and courteous service.

- **Community Room.** Midtown Bank provides a room for the community to use for meetings and special occasions. The room is available on a sign-up basis, and the customer should be directed to a customer service representative.

- **Special Services.** Fees are charged for the following special services:

| | |
|---|---|
| Photostatic Copy of Check | $2.00 per item |
| Preparation of Special Statement | $2.00 per statement |
| Reconciliation/Counseling | $20.00 per hour |
| Stop Payment Order | $15.00 per item |
| Check Returned for Insufficient Funds | $20.00 per check |

The bookkeeping department debits (charges) the customer's account for these special services.

# Handling Cash

We'll continue your training today by helping you learn how to handle cash (currency and coins) with confidence. There are certain skills and responsibilities involved in money handling. You are responsible for all cash that comes in and leaves your workstation. Each workday you must account for all money received or disbursed. You will be furnished a supply of coins and currency (paper money) for disbursing to customers during the banking day. This cash is kept in the vault for safekeeping after banking hours. You will verify the amount of money in your cash drawer at the beginning and the end of each banking day. As money accumulates during the day, any excess over $7,000 is transferred to the vault. When you have finished your training, you will use the Midtown Bank software to record cash transactions. The software will help in accounting for amounts and verifying the accuracy of your transactions.

## COUNTING AND PACKAGING MONEY

One money handling skill you must learn is how to count and package currency and coins. When counting currency, always stack all bills face up, top edge up. You will package currency in bundles (called **straps**) as indicated below.

| Bills per Strap | Denomination of Bills | | Amount per Strap |
|---|---|---|---|
| 50 | $100 | (hundreds) | $5,000 |
| 50 | 50 | (fifties) | 2,500 |
| 50 | 20 | (twenties) | 1,000 |
| 50 | 10 | (tens) | 500 |
| 50 | 5 | (fives) | 250 |
| 50 | 1 | (ones) | 50 |

Coins are counted and wrapped in rolls according to the following guidelines.

| Coins per Roll | Denomination of Coins | | Amount per Roll |
|---|---|---|---|
| 20 | $1.00 | (dollars) | $20.00 |
| 20 | .50 | (half dollars) | 10.00 |
| 40 | .25 | (quarters) | 10.00 |
| 50 | .10 | (dimes) | 5.00 |
| 40 | .05 | (nickels) | 2.00 |
| 50 | .01 | (pennies) | .50 |

Tellers are responsible for strapping their currency but are not required to wrap coins.

## THE COUNTERFEIT CURRENCY AND MONEY FACTS SEMINAR

All cash you receive from customers must be U.S. legal tender. Employees who handle money should be able to identify all bills quickly and discern whether or not they are legitimate. If anything about a bill looks different, such as the color, eyes, printing, or texture, you should compare it with other bills before you complete the transaction.

Because handling money is such an important part of your job, the Midtown Bank software includes a Counterfeit Currency and Money Facts Seminar. Follow these steps to attend the seminar:

1. Launch the Midtown Bank software.

2. Open your data file.

3. Pull down the Seminars menu and choose the Counterfeit Currency and Money Facts command.

4. Complete the seminar. You can print the seminar if you wish. Just click the Print button at the end of the seminar and click OK.

5. Save your file and exit the Midtown Bank software.

## RECEIVING AND DISBURSING CASH

In Work Assignment A for this unit, you will get some practice counting money. This is an especially important experience because you've worked only with checks and deposit tickets up to now. You'll be working inside the vault. Although we have a large sorting and counting machine, you will be working with smaller amounts at first, which you will sort and count by hand.

In a real-life situation you would be using actual money, but for this simulation you will use Simulated Cash Received Forms, Simulated Cash for Disbursement Forms, and Tally Sheets. The forms shown in the following illustrations will be used for all cash transactions in this simulation. You will use the numeric keypad in the Midtown Bank software to compute amounts and totals.

When you receive cash from a customer (represented by a completed Simulated Cash Received Form like the one shown in Figure IV.2), simply verify the amounts already listed to simulate counting the cash. Multiply the number of each denomination of money by its value to check for accuracy. For example, if the Simulated Cash Received Form shows three fifties, multiply three times fifty to check for accuracy. Key **5000** (entry will appear as 50.00) and press the plus (+) key to register. Then key **300** (entry will appear as 3.00) and press the multiplication (*) key to register. Press ENTER and the Midtown Bank keypad will show the product, 150.00. After you have checked all the multiplication, verify the addition to check the "Total Currency," "Total Coins," and "Total Cash Received" amounts.

**Figure IV.2**

*Simulated Cash*

*Received Form*

### SIMULATED CASH RECEIVED

**Currency:**

| | | | |
|---|---|---|---|
| 2 | Hundreds | $ | 200.00 |
| 1 | Fifties | $ | 50.00 |
| 16 | Twenties | $ | 320.00 |
| 39 | Tens | $ | 390.00 |
| 28 | Fives | $ | 140.00 |
| 44 | Ones | $ | 44.00 |

**Total Currency** $ 1,144.00

**Coins:**

| | | | |
|---|---|---|---|
| | Dollars | $ | |
| | Halves | $ | |
| 15 | Quarters | $ | 3.75 |
| 28 | Dimes | $ | 2.80 |
| 21 | Nickels | $ | 1.05 |
| 43 | Pennies | $ | .43 |

**Total Coins** $ 8.03

**TOTAL CASH RECEIVED** $ 1,152.03

(To Teller Drawer)

## CASH HANDLING RULES

**1.** Count cash received from a customer once.

**2.** Count cash disbursed to a customer twice.

**3.** Be on the alert for counterfeit money or money that is not U.S. legal tender.

**4.** Do not leave money lying on the counter.

**5.** Put cash away and lock it up before leaving the teller window.

**6.** Always finish one transaction before accepting another customer.

When you give cash to a customer, you will use a Simulated Cash for Disbursement Form. Write the number of bills and coins, then the dollar amount for each denomination used to equal the amount to be given to the bank customer. (A completed Simulated Cash for Disbursement Form is shown in Figure IV.3.) You may choose what denomination of bills and coins to give the customer as long as they equal the total amount to be disbursed. You should first ask the customer if she or he has a preference of denominations. For example, a customer may request several rolls of coins or may ask for a large number of small bills.

**Figure IV.3**

*Simulated Cash for Disbursement Form*

### SIMULATED CASH FOR DISBURSEMENT

**Currency:**

| | | |
|---|---|---|
| _1_ | Hundreds | $ _100.00_ |
| | Fifties | $ |
| _5_ | Twenties | $ _100.00_ |
| _5_ | Tens | $ _50.00_ |
| _3_ | Fives | $ _15.00_ |
| _4_ | Ones | $ _4.00_ |

**Total Currency**     $ _269.00_

**Coins:**

| | | |
|---|---|---|
| | Dollars | $ |
| | Halves | $ |
| _1_ | Quarters | $ _.25_ |
| _1_ | Dimes | $ _.10_ |
| _1_ | Nickels | $ _.05_ |
| _3_ | Pennies | $ _.03_ |

**Total Coins**     $ _.43_

**TOTAL CASH DISBURSED**     $ _269.43_

(To Customer)

If straps or rolls are received or disbursed, refer to page 45 to determine how much money is included in each roll or strap. Then, simply multiply the number of straps or rolls times the money amount.

You will use a Tally Sheet like the one shown in Figure IV.4 to simulate keeping track of all the money in your cash drawer. The Tally Sheet will reflect what you started with at the beginning of the day, all of the cash transactions going into and

# TALLY SHEET

DATE _____

| (1) $ Denominations | (2) Total Cash Brought Forward | (3) Transactions + or − | | | | | | | | | | | | | | (4) = Total $ |
|---|---|---|---|---|---|---|---|---|---|---|---|---|---|---|---|---|
| | | A | B | | | | | | | | | | | | | |
| BILLS: Hundreds $100 | | +200 | −100 | | | | | | | | | | | | | |
| Fifties $50 | | +50 | | | | | | | | | | | | | | |
| Twenties $20 | | +320 | −100 | | | | | | | | | | | | | |
| Tens $10 | | +390 | −50 | | | | | | | | | | | | | |
| Fives $5 | | +140 | −15 | | | | | | | | | | | | | |
| Ones $1 | | +44 | −4 | | | | | | | | | | | | | |
| COINS: Dollars $1 | | | | | | | | | | | | | | | | |
| Halves .50 | | | | | | | | | | | | | | | | |
| Quarters .25 | | +3.75 | −.25 | | | | | | | | | | | | | |
| Dimes .10 | | +2.80 | −.10 | | | | | | | | | | | | | |
| Nickels .05 | | +1.05 | −.05 | | | | | | | | | | | | | |
| Pennies .01 | | +.43 | −.03 | | | | | | | | | | | | | |

| | |
|---|---|
| (5) Total Cash | |
| (6) Minus (−) Amount Transferred to Vault Account at Closing | |
| (7) Cash Brought Forward | |

**Figure IV.4**

*Tally Sheet*

out of the drawer during the day, and the cash remaining at the end of the business day. Study Figure IV.4 as the sections of the Tally Sheet are described.

1. This section is a list of the denominations (kinds) of money and their value.

2. This section shows the dollar amount of bills and coins in your cash drawer at the beginning of the banking day.

3. Section 3 has separate columns for each cash transaction. The total dollar amount for each transaction is listed by denomination. Be careful to indicate *adding* with a "+" for cash received and *subtracting* with a "−" for cash disbursed in these columns.

4. In Section 4, the dollar amounts are totaled horizontally beginning with Column 2 by adding or subtracting for each denomination.

5. This section is the total of the dollar amounts in Section 4.

6. This is the dollar amount over $5,000 to be transferred to the Vault Account at closing.

7. This section shows cash brought forward for the next day.

The dollar amounts of bills and coins listed on the Simulated Cash Received Form, Figure IV.2, and the Simulated Cash for Disbursement Form, Figure IV.3, are entered in Columns A and B on the Tally Sheet shown in Figure IV.4. At the end of the day, you will complete Sections 4, 5, 6, and 7 of the Tally Sheet. The amount in Section 5 should be the amount of money in your cash drawer.

You have two different types of Work Assignments for today. In Work Assignment A, you will practice receiving and disbursing cash using simulated cash forms and a Tally Sheet. You will use the Midtown Bank software in this assignment to prove your work is accurate. This is called **balancing** . In Work Assignment B, you will practice answering some customer requests. Follow the instructions in the Unit IV Work Assignments to complete your work for the day.

# Work Assignment A                           Unit IV

**Instructions:** *Continue your time worked record. You will be completing simulated cash forms and a Tally Sheet and will use the Midtown Bank software to balance. You will make no entries to the computer cash account for this activity.*

1. Remove and separate at the perforations the ten simulated cash forms labeled A through J and the Tally Sheet labeled IV from the back of this *Employee Manual*.

2. Launch the Midtown Bank software and open your data file. Choose the Keypad command from the Options menu.

3. Complete all counting activities for the ten simulated cash forms. Verify amounts on all Cash Received Forms, correcting errors, if any. Complete all Cash for Disbursement Forms.

4. Enter the information from the cash forms in consecutive order on the Tally Sheet.

5. Complete the Tally Sheet.

6. Use the software and the numeric keypad on your computer to enter (add) all final totals from Simulated Cash Received Forms and subtract final totals from Simulated Cash for Disbursement Forms. Then total.

7. If the total is the same as the Total Cash in Section 5 on the Tally Sheet, your work is perfect. If the total does not equal the total on the Tally Sheet, you need to recount your money (check your calculations) and make corrections on the forms and Tally Sheet when you find errors. You will have to recheck your work until you have corrected all errors and these two totals are the same.

When you are responsible for a workstation, you will use a similar procedure in handling and balancing your cash. You might occasionally make some errors in the course of a day's work. You may find the errors yourself; but, fortunately, your computer will keep an accumulative total of your transactions and the bank's proof department further verifies each transaction.

When you have balanced, fasten the simulated cash forms and Tally Sheet to this Work Assignment and submit them to your instructor.

# Work Assignment B

**Unit IV**

**Instructions:** *So you can practice answering customer requests, several customer requests are provided in this Work Assignment. Read each request, then provide the information desired. If specific information is requested, complete the Customer Request for Information Form provided with the request. If general information is requested, answer briefly in the space provided. Refer to pages 42-44 for information concerning customer identification and bank services. You may access the Midtown Bank software for information. (Remember that you are still working at Midtown Bank's Drive-thru window.) As you handle each request, think how you can be thorough, helpful, and courteous in this important duty. From this point forward, you need to click Yes when you are asked if you want to advance the bookmarking. The only time you will click No to this request is if you accidentally access the wrong account. When you have completed the customer requests, submit the Work Assignment B pages to your instructor for evaluation. Be sure to save your work and exit the software properly when you have finished the Work Assignments.*

## CUSTOMER REQUEST 1

**Customer:** Hello, I'm Patrick O'Sullivan. We have a checking account here. Can you tell me if our recent deposit has been cleared yet?

**Employee:** What is your account number?

**Customer:** I'm sorry, I don't know it yet.

**Employee:** I can look it up for you. What was the amount of the deposit?

**Customer:** I believe it was about $914.

**Employee:** I'll see if the deposit has cleared.

**REQUEST FOR CUSTOMER INFORMATION**

**Name** _____

**Acct. No.** _____

**Acct. Type** _____

**Last Deposit** _____

**Comments** _____

_____

_____

## CUSTOMER REQUEST 2

**Customer:** I wonder if you can tell me what my checking account balance is.

**Employee:** May I have your name and account number please?

**Customer:** My name is Joyce Brucker and my account number is 349-589-6.

**Employee:** Please give me the amount of your last deposit for identification purposes.

**Customer:** It was $78.

**Employee:** Thank you.

**REQUEST FOR CUSTOMER INFORMATION**

**Name** _____

**Acct. No.** _____

**Acct. Type** _____

**Last Deposit** _____

**Comments** _____

_____

_____

## CUSTOMER REQUEST 3

**Customer:** Hello. I'm Patricia Bowers. I wonder if you could see if check number 301 has come back in, and tell me what the amount was if it's there. I forgot to write it in my checkbook.

**Employee:** What is the amount of your last deposit?

**Customer:** $750.00.

**Employee:** Just a moment. I'll get that information for you.

---

**REQUEST FOR CUSTOMER INFORMATION**

**Name** _____

**Acct. No.** _____

**Acct. Type** _____

**Last Deposit** _____

**Comments** _____

_____

_____

---

## CUSTOMER REQUEST 4

**Customer:** I want to open a new checking account. Can you do that here?

**Employee:** _____

_____

_____

_____

_____

---

## CUSTOMER REQUEST 5

**Customer:** Would it be very expensive to have someone help me get my checkbook straightened out? My dad is going to disown me if I don't quit writing checks that come back.

**Employee:** _____

_____

_____

_____

_____

---

## CUSTOMER REQUEST 6

**Customer:** I saw your ad in the paper about your automobile loans. What do I have to do to get one of them? How much interest do you charge?

**Employee:** _____

_____

_____

_____

_____

# Unit Check Activity

## Unit IV

**Instructions:** *Circle the word(s) that will correctly complete the following sentences. You may refer to Unit IV as needed. When you are finished, remove and submit your completed Unit Check to your instructor for evaluation.*

1. At night, all money is placed in the (cash drawer, vault) for safekeeping.

2. Currency is packed together in bundles called (rolls, straps).

3. When deposited, coins are rolled and (strapped, wrapped) according to denomination.

4. A teller can verify whether sufficient money is available for check cashing by consulting the (computer customer accounts, signature record files).

5. Customers see (bookkeepers, tellers) more than any other bank employees.

6. To verify a customer's identity before giving account information, a teller asks for the amount and the date of the last (request, deposit) made to the bank.

7. (Customer counseling, Depositing money) can cost the customer as much as $20.00 an hour.

8. When counting money, look for the face of (George Washington, Alexander Hamilton) on ten dollar bills.

9. Quarters are rolled in wrappers of (50, 40) each.

10. When you disburse cash, you should (add to, subtract from) your cash drawer.

11. When you receive a cash deposit from a customer, you should (add to, subtract from) your cash drawer.

12. Bank employees reveal account information (to any family member of the true owner, only to the true owner) of an account.

13. The bank's (customer service, proof) department verifies all teller transactions.

14. Traveler's checks, cashier's checks, and money orders are (negotiable instruments, deposits).

15. A teller's most frequent activity is (answering telephone requests, handling cash).

# TELLER
# PROCEDURES

## Objectives

At the completion of Unit V, you will be able to:

- Safeguard cash properly.
- React appropriately in the event of a robbery or other emergency situation.
- Understand work flow at a bank teller workstation.
- Complete and use various forms for daily teller activities.
- Arrange the teller work area for counter top activities.
- Complete workstation and computer activities for specific types of customer transactions.
- Complete a day's activity as a teller trainee.

# Learning to Handle Emergencies

Before you begin working as a teller, you need to learn the procedures Midtown Bank uses to safeguard money and to protect bank employees in emergency situations. The Security and Emergency Procedures seminar on the Midtown Bank software explains what you should do in an emergency. Follow these steps to attend the seminar:

1. Launch the Midtown Bank Software.

2. Open your data file.

3. Pull down the Seminars menu and choose the Security and Emergency Procedures command.

4. Complete the seminar (read the information on the screen). If you want to print the seminar, click the Print button at the end of the seminar. When the Print dialog box appears, click OK.

5. Save your data file.

6. Exit the Midtown Bank software.

# Tracking the Activity at the Teller Window

A teller's work can be compared to directing traffic. Cash, checks, deposit tickets, and other forms are sent in four directions:

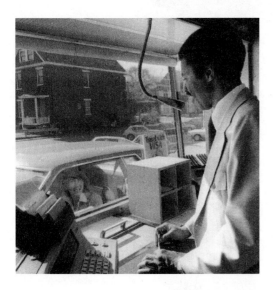

1. **To the Teller Window (or Workstation).** All documents and forms needed to handle customer transactions are at the teller workstation.

2. **To the Cash Drawer.** All money passes through the cash drawer, including cash brought forward (a set amount of cash at the beginning of each day to be used to make change and disbursements to customers), cash deposited by customers, and cash disbursed during the banking day. At the end of each working day, tellers must account for their cash transactions. Cash is stored in the cash drawer and placed in the bank vault at the end of the day. Banks often disburse more cash than they receive; therefore, they periodically purchase large amounts of wrapped and strapped money from the Federal Reserve System.

3. **To Customers.** Customers may receive cash, deposit receipts, or other documents, depending on the specific transaction.

4. **To the Proof Department.** A bank must safeguard and accurately account for its customers' money. Tellers send all checks, deposit tickets, and completed Transaction Request Forms to the proof department, where they are verified, corrected if errors are found, and then distributed for final processing to customer accounts. **Note:** In this simulation you will be working with

realistic checks and other negotiable instruments, deposit tickets, and Transaction Request Forms. All cash transactions will be simulated using Simulated Cash Received and Cash for Disbursement Forms and a Tally Sheet.

Tellers in our branch are on-line with the central office of Midtown Bank, where the bookkeeping and proof departments are located. This means that all customer transactions can be entered directly into the individual accounts from the teller workstation. You will use the Midtown Bank software to make these entries. The numeric keypad in the software will allow you to do your calculations quickly and accurately. Although you will still use many paper forms in your teller job, computer software simplifies your daily activities.

# ■ Procedures and Forms for the Teller Workstation

Midtown Bank uses certain forms and has developed specific procedures for you to follow in your daily teller activities. You have already learned about many of these forms and procedures in your training. Today, you'll receive some additional information regarding the procedures you will follow when you assume your teller duties.

## CASH IN AND CASH OUT

When you receive cash from a customer (cash in) or disburse (give) cash to a customer (cash out), you must make an entry in the Midtown Bank software Cash Drawer Account. This will help you keep track of the money handled during the day so you will be able to balance the cash at the end of the day. The Cash Drawer Account shows a cumulative total of the cash in the drawer and lists each cash transaction. Your final (net) cash total in the Cash Drawer Account should equal the amount of cash you have counted at the end of the day, as shown on a Tally Sheet.

## STOPPING PAYMENT OF CHECKS

Sometimes a bank customer writes a check and then decides that she or he does not want the bank to pay it. When this happens, the customer can request the bank to stop payment of the check. This request should be made soon enough to ensure that the check will not be paid. A customer service representative processes a stop payment form that describes the check and authorizes the stop payment. The customer must sign this form, either in person at the time it is completed or as soon as possible after the information is given by telephone. Midtown Bank charges customers for this service. (See the chart on page 44 in Unit IV.)

Our tellers direct customers wishing to stop payment on a check to a customer service representative to complete or sign the stop payment form. If there is a stop payment of a check for an account, it appears in the Customer Account window of the Midtown Bank software. You are responsible for obeying the stop payment order, so you should examine accounts carefully for these orders before cashing checks. You can check the status of a stop payment request at your workstation by accessing the customer's account on the Midtown Bank software.

## TRANSACTION REQUEST FORM

A Transaction Request Form (shown in Figure V.1) is a multipurpose form used at the teller workstation for any of the following transactions:

1. All cash withdrawals from savings accounts.

2. Cash withdrawals from checking accounts. (A customer may use this form for cash instead of a personalized check.)

3. All deposits to savings accounts.

4. Deposits to checking accounts. (A customer may use this form instead of a personalized deposit ticket.)

5. Transfer of funds from one account to another, such as from savings to checking.

---

### TRANSACTION REQUEST FORM

**Midtown Bank**
Dallas, Texas

Name _____      Date _____

Account # _____      Teller _____

**DEPOSIT**     Acct. Type: Checking ☐  Savings ☐

| Cash | | |
| Checks | | |
| | | |
| | | |
| | | |
| | | |
| Total Received | | |
| Less Cash Received | | |
| Net Deposit | | |

**WITHDRAWAL**

Checking    $_____
Savings     $_____

**TRANSFER**

$_____
From Acct. # _____
To Acct. # _____

Signature _____

**Figure V. I**

*Transaction*

*Request Form*

Notice the signature portion of the form. You must always secure the customer's signature if a cash disbursement transaction or a transfer is involved. You also must access the customer's account to verify that sufficient funds are available before withdrawing any cash using this form. You will use the Midtown Bank software to enter the transaction in the customer's account.

## TRANSFERRING EXCESS CASH FROM CASH DRAWER TO VAULT

Periodically during the day, you must check the balance of the Cash Drawer Account. The balance in your cash drawer should not exceed $7,000. If the balance exceeds $7,000, you need to transfer the excess funds to the vault. Use these steps to make the transfer:

1. Determine the amount to be transferred. To do this, subtract the maximum allowable cash ($7,000) from the amount in the cash drawer. If your answer is a negative number, then you have less than $7,000 in your cash drawer and you do not need to transfer anything. If your answer is a positive number, then you need to transfer that amount to the vault.

**2.** In the Cash Drawer Account window of the Midtown Bank software, subtract the amount to be transferred. Close the Cash Drawer Account window. (Be sure you remember the amount you are transferring.)

**3.** Open the Vault Account window by clicking the Vault icon or by pulling down the Accounts menu and choosing the Vault command. Add the amount you are transferring to the Vault Account.

**4.** Ask your supervisor to accompany you to take the cash to the vault. Simulate this process by clicking on the supervisor desk in the lobby of the Midtown Bank software. A message will appear in a dialog box on the screen; click OK to continue working after the message appears.

## BALANCING CASH

After the bank closes for the day, you must account for the accuracy of all *cash* transactions. Some banks do all balancing on the computer. Midtown Bank uses a combination of computer and manual activities. Follow these steps to account for the accuracy of your cash transactions:

**1.** Count all the cash in your cash drawer (use the Tally Sheet and Cash Received and Cash for Disbursement Forms). This cash total will include the cash in your drawer at the beginning of the day, plus any cash given by customers, less any cash you have disbursed to customers, and less any excess cash you have transferred to the Vault Account during the day.

**2.** Access the Cash Drawer Activity report in the Midtown Bank software and print it. (Click the Print button at the bottom of the report.)

**3.** Compare the totals from Steps 1 and 2. These totals are called **proof totals**. If the two proof totals are the same, your work is perfect and your cash transactions balance. If your cash transactions do not balance (the proof totals are not the same), use one or more of the following steps to balance cash:

- Find the exact amount of the difference. Are you over or short?

- Recount the cash.

- Verify that you recorded all the cash transactions in the Cash Drawer Account.

- If necessary, recheck all customer cash transactions for the day. Look for errors on simulated cash forms and for errors in the amounts entered in the Cash Drawer Account.

- Enlist help from your supervisor if you are unable to find your errors.

- Write the amount you are short or over on your Cash Drawer Activity report if you still cannot find all the errors.

**4.** Transfer all excess cash (cash over the beginning balance of $5,000 each day) to the Vault Account. Use your numeric keypad to determine the amount to transfer (cash drawer balance minus the beginning cash drawer balance of $5,000). If your ending cash balance is less than $5,000, you will not need to make a transfer. Write on your Tally Sheet how much you are transferring to the Vault Account. Then follow Steps 2 and 3 at the top of page 59 to complete this transaction.

**5.** Print a Daily Account Activity report and a Cash Drawer Activity report. Sign your name beneath your printed name on the computer printouts.

**Note:** An actual bank teller may not be able to print all the transactions for the day, but the Midtown Bank software automatically lists all transactions made to customer accounts. You can print this list at any time to help you check the accuracy of your work or as required by your supervisor.

### CLOSING ACTIVITY

After the cash has been counted and balanced, ask your supervisor to initial the Cash Drawer Activity report. Then, place your cash drawer in the bank vault for safekeeping. All documents used to complete customer transactions (checks and other negotiable instruments, deposits, and Transaction Request Forms) should be placed in your Proof Department/Supervisor envelope and forwarded to the proof department through your supervisor.

# ◼ Teller Activities

On a typical day, you will arrange your working area to include all the forms and documents needed to handle customer transactions and prepare to greet your first customer. Most transactions at your window will fall into one of these categories: receiving deposits from customers and disbursing cash to customers. You will use the Midtown Bank software to post these transactions to customers' accounts. You will handle both checking and savings account transactions.

Your training is almost completed, and you will soon be assuming your duties at a teller window. The following sections explain in detail how to perform your daily activities at your workstation counter and on the computer. Remember, all counter and computer activities for one customer transaction must be complete before you serve another customer. It is very important for you to read and follow these instructions exactly; otherwise, you could lose your work.

### RECEIVING DEPOSITS

General rules for receiving all checking and savings deposits are as follows:

**1.** Verify all entries on the deposit ticket.

**2.** Be sure that the account number is on the deposit ticket. If it is not, use the Midtown Bank software to get the account number.

**3.** Examine each check for proper endorsement. (See Unit III.)

**4.** Be sure none of the checks are postdated. (See Unit III.)

**5.** Count all money carefully.

**6.** For this simulation, you should sign for the customer when a signature is needed. Because of this special circumstance, your signature does not need to match the authorized one. Keep in mind that in a real banking environment the signatures must match.

## CHECKS ONLY DEPOSITS

When a deposit (either checking or savings) consists of checks only, follow these steps to process the transaction:

1. After verifying all entries, initial the total on the original personalized deposit ticket or on the Transaction Request Form to indicate that the amount is correct.

2. Click the Customer Accounts icon or pull down the Accounts menu and choose the Customer command. Follow the procedures you learned previously to access the customer's account.

3. Click the Deposit radio button in the Transaction Type box. Enter the amount of the deposit in the Deposit Amount field of the Customer Account window and then click Enter. If you make a mistake, immediately click Undo to remove the entry. When you are finished entering data, click OK. Advance the bookmarking.

4. Use a paper clip to fasten the deposit ticket to the check(s). These items are sent to the proof department. (To simulate this, place the documents in the Proof Department/Supervisor envelope.)

## CASH ONLY DEPOSITS

When a deposit consists of cash only, follow these steps to complete the transaction:

1. Count the money and compare the total with the amount shown on the customer's prepared deposit ticket (either personalized deposit ticket or prepared Transaction Request Form).

   ■ Recheck the coin and currency amounts shown on the deposit ticket.

   ■ Initial the total on the deposit ticket to indicate that the amount listed is correct.

   Remember, all cash transactions will be simulated by using Cash Received or Cash for Disbursement Forms along with a Tally Sheet.

2. Click the Customer Accounts icon or pull down the Accounts menu and choose the Customer command. Follow the procedures you learned previously to access the customer's account.

3. Click the Deposit radio button in the Transaction Type box. Enter the amount of the deposit in the Deposit Amount field of the Customer Account window and then click Enter. If you make a mistake, immediately click Undo to remove the entry. When you are finished entering data, click OK. Advance the bookmarking.

4. Make sure the cash drawer is unlocked. Click the Cash Drawer icon or pull down the Accounts menu and choose the Cash Drawer command. Enter the amount of cash received in the Amount field, and then click Enter. When you are finished entering data, click OK.

5. Place the cash from the customer in the teller cash drawer. (Simulate this by recording the information on a Cash Received Form and Tally Sheet.)

6. The deposit ticket goes to the proof department. (Place it in your Proof Department/Supervisor envelope.)

## CHECKS AND CASH DEPOSITS

When a deposit consists of both checks and cash, follow these steps:

1. Count the cash and examine the checks and total shown on the deposit ticket or Transaction Request Form. Use the general rules on page 60 for this process.

2. Initial the total on the deposit ticket to indicate that the amount listed is correct.

3. Click the Customer Accounts icon or pull down the Accounts menu and choose the Customer command. Follow the procedures you learned previously to access the customer's account.

4. Click the Deposit radio button in the Transaction Type box. Enter the amount of the deposit in the Deposit Amount field of the Customer Account window and then click Enter. If you make a mistake, immediately click Undo to remove the entry. When you are finished entering data, click OK. Advance the bookmarking.

5. Make sure the cash drawer is unlocked. Click the Cash Drawer icon or pull down the Accounts menu and choose the Cash Drawer command. Enter the amount of cash received in the Amount field, and then click Enter. When you are finished entering data, click OK.

6. Place the cash in the teller cash drawer. (Simulate this activity by using a Cash Received Form and Tally Sheet.)

7. Attach the deposit ticket to the check(s). These items go to the proof department. (Place them in the Proof Department/Supervisor envelope.)

## DISBURSING CASH

General requirements for disbursing money either for checks written for Cash or for cash withdrawals from savings accounts are as follows:

1. Cash checks for Midtown Bank accounts *only*. Either the drawer or the payee must be a Midtown Bank account owner.

2. Cash checks or withdraw money from a savings or checking account only if the customer's account balance is sufficient to cover the check or savings withdrawal.

3. Verify the signature of the drawer by asking for proper identification or by checking the signature record. If you do not personally know the customer, compare the driver's license signature with the check signature and verify the driver's license number by accessing the customer's account in the Midtown Bank software. If you are still unsure, you may need to have the signature faxed from another location.

4. Be sure the amounts in numbers and words are the same and are legible.

5. If checks are not made payable to Midtown Bank or Cash, see if they are properly endorsed.

6. If the date is later than the current date (postdated), do not cash the check.

7. If you are not certain the check satisfies all of the requirements, ask an officer of the bank to approve the check before you cash it. If an officer is not available, explain to the customer the bank's policy that prohibits cashing the check.

## CASHING CHECKS AND CASH WITHDRAWALS FROM SAVINGS

Follow these steps to withdraw cash from a customer savings or checking account:

1. Follow the general requirements for examining checks and disbursing cash to customers.

2. For a savings withdrawal, prepare the savings withdrawal portion of a Transaction Request Form and obtain the customer's signature. Be sure to initial the form.

3. Click the Customer Accounts icon or pull down the Accounts menu and choose the Customer command. Follow the procedures you learned previously to access the customer's account. Verify that the customer has enough money in the account to complete the transaction.

4. Click the Withdrawal radio button in the Transaction Type box. Enter the amount of the withdrawal in the Withdraw Amount field of the Customer Account window and then click Enter. (Remember, you can always click Undo to correct any mistakes.) When you are finished entering data, click OK. Advance the bookmarking.

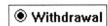

5. Make sure the cash drawer is unlocked. Click the Cash Drawer icon or pull down the Accounts menu and choose the Cash Drawer command. Enter the amount of cash withdrawn in the Amount field (include a minus sign at the end of the amount to indicate a withdrawal), and then click Enter. When you are finished entering data, click OK.

6. Count out the amount of cash indicated on the check or on the savings withdrawal portion of the Transaction Request Form.

7. Give the cash to the customer. (Simulate this activity by using a Cash for Disbursement Form and Tally Sheet.)

8. Send the check or the Transaction Request Form to the proof department. (Place the relevant materials in the Proof Department/Supervisor envelope.)

## LESS CASH RECEIVED DEPOSITS

When a customer presents a check or other negotiable instrument for deposit but also wants some cash, follow these steps:

1. Examine the check for proper endorsement.

2. Verify all entries shown on the deposit ticket or on the Transaction Request Form.

3. Have the customer sign the deposit ticket or the Transaction Request Form.

4. Initial the deposit ticket or the Transaction Request Form to indicate that the total is correct.

5. Click the Customer Accounts icon or pull down the Accounts menu and choose the Customer command. Follow the procedures you learned previously to access the customer's account.

6. Click the Deposit radio button in the Transaction Type box. Enter the amount of the deposit in the Deposit Amount field of the Customer Account window and then click Enter. (Remember, you can always click Undo to correct any mistakes.) When you are finished entering data, click OK. Advance the bookmarking.

**7.** Make sure the cash drawer is unlocked. Click the Cash Drawer icon or pull down the Accounts menu and choose the Cash Drawer command. Enter the amount of cash withdrawn in the Amount field (include a minus sign at the end of the amount to indicate a withdrawal), and then click Enter. When you are finished entering data, click OK.

**8.** Count out the amount of cash indicated opposite "Less Cash Received" on the deposit ticket or on the Transaction Request Form.

**9.** Give the cash to the customer. (Simulate this activity by using a Cash for Disbursement Form and Tally Sheet.)

**10.** Attach the deposit ticket or the Transaction Request Form to the check(s). These items go to the proof department. (Place them in the Proof Department/ Supervisor envelope.)

## TRANSFER OF MONEY FROM ONE CUSTOMER ACCOUNT TO ANOTHER ACCOUNT

No cash handling actually takes place when money is transferred from a savings account to a checking account or from a checking account to a savings account. However, you must complete some forms and make some computer entries. Follow these steps to complete this type of transaction:

**1.** Prepare the transfer portion of a Transaction Request Form showing the amount to be transferred and the accounts involved.

**2.** Obtain the customer's signature on the form. Be sure to initial the form.

**3.** Click the Customer Accounts icon or pull down the Accounts menu and choose the Customer command. Follow the procedures you learned previously to access the customer's account. Because there are two accounts involved, be sure you access the account from which money will be withdrawn. Verify that the customer has sufficient funds to complete the transaction.

**4.** Click the Transfer radio button in the Transaction Type box. Check the Transfer box at the right side of the screen to make sure the radio buttons indicate the correct "From" and "To" accounts. If they are incorrect, correct them now. Enter the appropriate account numbers. Enter the amount of the transfer in the Transfer Amount field of the Customer Account window and then click Enter. (Remember, you can always click Undo to correct any mistakes.) When you are finished entering data, click OK. Advance the bookmarking.

**5.** Send the Transaction Request Form to the proof department. (Place the relevant materials in the Proof Department/Supervisor envelope.)

## DEPOSIT OF CASH FROM CHECKING ACCOUNT DEPOSIT INTO SAVINGS ACCOUNT

The Less Cash Received portion of the deposit ticket or Transaction Request Form is used to remove cash from a deposit amount. The cash is given to the customer who in turn deposits the cash into his or her savings account. Follow these steps to complete the transaction:

**1.** Have the customer sign the deposit ticket or Transaction Request Form.

2. Verify the information on all documents and initial the deposit ticket or Transaction Request Form.

3. Click the Customer Accounts icon or pull down the Accounts menu and choose the Customer command. Follow the procedures you learned previously to access the customer's checking account.

4. Click the Deposit radio button in the Transaction Type box. Enter the amount of the deposit in the Deposit Amount field of the Customer Account window and then click Enter. (Remember, you can always click Undo to correct any mistakes.) When you are finished entering data, click OK. Advance the bookmarking.

5. Make sure the cash drawer is unlocked. Click the Cash Drawer icon or pull down the Accounts menu and choose the Cash Drawer command. Enter the amount of cash withdrawn in the Amount field (include a minus sign at the end of the amount to indicate a withdrawal), and then click Enter. (Remember, you can correct a mistake by clicking Undo.) When you are finished entering data, click OK.

6. Give the customer the cash requested. (Use a Simulated Cash for Disbursement Form and enter on Tally Sheet.)

7. Complete the deposit to savings portion of a Transaction Request Form.

8. The customer will return the cash to you. Count the cash received for this deposit. (Use a Simulated Cash Received Form and enter on Tally Sheet.)

9. Access the customer's savings account in the Midtown Bank software and record the deposit amount. Advance the bookmarking.

10. Access the Cash Drawer window in the Midtown Bank software and record the cash deposit amount.

11. Send the appropriate documents to the proof department. (Place them in the Proof Department/Supervisor envelope.)

## MAKING CHANGE FOR A CUSTOMER

To make change for a customer, simply exchange one denomination of cash for another. This is an even exchange, so you do not need to make any computer entries. Follow these steps to simulate the process:

1. Verify the amounts on the Simulated Cash Received Form.

2. Complete a Simulated Cash for Disbursement Form for an equal amount of money in denominations of your or the customer's choice.

3. Enter the information from both forms on the Tally Sheet.

## COMPUTER PROBLEMS

Occasionally, your computer will be "down" and you will not be able to enter items into customers' or cash accounts immediately. You should continue to serve customers. Simply fill out the usual forms and proceed with all workstation activities. Inform customers that you will enter transactions as soon as possible after computer service is restored. You may have to delay making these entries until the bank has closed if you are very busy at your workstation. Don't forget to make entries to the Cash Drawer Account.

## DAILY CLOSING ACTIVITIES

Each day you will follow these steps to close your teller window:

1. Complete daily balancing of cash as outlined on pages 59-60.

2. Transfer excess cash from your Cash Drawer Account to the Vault Account. (See pages 58-59.)

3. Generate the following reports using the Midtown Bank software:

   ■ Daily Account Activity report

   ■ Cash Drawer Activity report

4. Bundle all documents and reports used to complete the customer transactions and forward them to the proof department through your supervisor. (Place the relevant materials in the Proof Department/Supervisor envelope.)

5. Save your file and exit the Midtown Bank software.

6. Organize supplies and equipment neatly at your workstation.

## ■ Your First Time at a Teller Window

You've completed your teller training and are now ready to serve bank customers. You have been assigned to the drive-thru window because customer traffic is slower there than in our lobby area. Refer to your *Employee Manual* or your computer Help menu, or ask for assistance if you need more information. As your supervisor, I'll be observing you today as you begin to work on your own.

First, you should organize your work area. You will need the following forms and supplies near your computer for convenience:

1. **Envelopes.** You learned about the logistics of your work flow in this unit. To simulate the activities described, place items in the two envelopes included with this *Employee Manual*. The envelopes are labeled "Teller/Miscellaneous" and "Proof Department/Supervisor." Throughout the simulation, you will not actually give any items (deposit receipts, cash, and so on) to the customer. Instead, you will place items in the Proof Department/Supervisor envelope for your supervisor to review. The Teller/Miscellaneous envelope will be used for documents that do not need to be turned in to your supervisor (simulated cash forms and Tally Sheets), working papers removed from this *Employee Manual* but not yet completed, and documents that are returned to you by your supervisor.

2. **Blank Forms and Working Papers.** Each transaction in the Work Assignment is a dialogue with a bank customer. The dialogue is preceded by a job number. All jobs in this unit are preceded by Roman numeral V. You will remove from the back of this *Employee Manual* all working papers and documents with the corresponding job number before you serve that bank customer. Be sure that you have all of the working papers for a particular job number, as the documents do not always appear in exact numeric order. Whenever possible, remove working papers for only one job at a time. Do not remove the forms until you need them. When removing working papers for one job, it may be necessary to tear out the working papers for a future job. If this is the case, set aside the torn out working papers until needed. If your class period ends before you have processed all removed working papers, store any unused working papers in the envelope labeled "Teller/Miscellaneous" until your next class period.

3. **Miscellaneous Supplies.** You'll need several paper clips, a pen, and a pencil. You may also want to have a file folder available for keeping various working papers.

Remember, you'll be using simulated cash forms and a Tally Sheet instead of real money. As you simulate receiving and disbursing cash, enter the dollar amount received or given on the Tally Sheet as you make each transaction. Use the blocks below "Transactions" in Section 3 of the Tally Sheet to enter the job number of each transaction involving cash. This will help you later if you need to find an error in your calculations. The job numbers you enter will not be consecutive because all transactions will not involve cash handling. Section 2 shows the cash in your cash drawer at the beginning of your day.

If a customer's signature is needed, simulate this by signing the appropriate signature yourself. For example, you will need to sign signatures for endorsements, less cash deposits, and transfers.

You can review all procedures for transactions by consulting the Midtown Bank software Help menu or by referring to your *Employee Manual*. You should now be ready to begin your Unit V Work Assignment and your first time at a teller window.

# *Work Assignment*                                           *Unit V*

**Instructions:** *Today is May 17. Continue your time worked record. Launch the Midtown Bank software and open your data file. Then, click the Drive-thru Window hot spot to get started working. Next, unlock the cash drawer. You can either click the Lock icon, click the Cash Drawer hot spot, or pull down the Options menu and choose the Lock command to lock or unlock the cash drawer. (See Appendix A or Help for further information.) Remember to lock the cash drawer whenever you leave the teller window and when you are finished for the day.*

*Be sure to read and follow the messages in the text and message boxes on the screen. Don't forget to check for important messages at the bottom of the customer transactions list. Also remember to double-check the type of account being accessed; some customers have more than one account with Midtown Bank. If you accidentally access the wrong account, just cancel the transaction and **do not** advance the bookmarking.*

*Consider how you will respond to your customers—what you will say and do. Use the space below each dialogue to make any notes about the transaction or to write any questions you want to ask your supervisor.*

*Are you ready to begin the day? That man in the blue van looks a little impatient, doesn't he?*

## Job No.

**V-1**     Good morning. I guess my clock was wrong. I've been waiting ten minutes for you to open. I need to deposit these checks.


**V-2**     Hi. I just want to cash this check. I don't want any new ones.

**V-3**     Will this deposit get posted to my account right away?

**V-4**     I want to make a deposit to my savings. Can you tell me what my new balance will be?

**V-5**     Can you change this $100 bill for me? I'd like it all in small bills.

**V-6**     Hello. You're new here, aren't you? Martha's usually at this window. Is she on vacation?

**V-7**     May I cash this check?

**V-8**     Oh! You startled me. I'm still half asleep. It was late when we closed last night. I need to make a deposit.

**V-9**     I want to get rid of all this cash. I finally had my garage sale last weekend. I can't believe I made so much—I've had some of those things for years. I guess I'll just put it in my savings account.

**V-10**     I need to keep a little cash out of this check. My wife and I are going over to Fort Worth tomorrow.

**V-11**  Can I make a savings withdrawal here at the drive-thru window? I would hate to go inside looking the way I do. I'd like to withdraw $275. I'm not sure of my account number. I'd like to have mostly $20 bills. Oh, I really am forgetful this morning—my account is in the name of Carlos M. or Veronica Viviano.

**V-12**  My, it's really hot today, isn't it? Thanks.

**V-13**  I worked for Mrs. Goodman today and she gave me this check. Will you cash it for me? It's on your bank. Do I need to sign it or anything?

**Note:** This is a special kind of transaction. The check won't actually clear right away, so the account will not reflect the normal "Check Paid" indication after the transaction is processed. Instead, the transaction will show up as a withdrawal, just as if the customer withdrew cash from the account. The check will actually clear later in the month.

**V-14**  Hello. I'd like to transfer $500 from my savings account to my checking account. This is my little grandson. I notice you've been giving lollipops to the little ones. He says he wants a red one if you have it. My name is Holly Conley.

**V-15**  I need to stop payment on a check. Can you do that for me here? I hope so.

**V-16**  I'd like to deposit these checks. By the way, can you tell me what my new balance will be?

**V-17**  I want to cash this check. Can you find out if check number 863 has cleared my account? I wrote it about a month ago.

**V-18**  Hello. I'm a little late getting here this morning. We really had a busy day yesterday and we've been training a new cashier, too.

**V-19**  Oh—hello.

**V-20**  My, this is really good service. Is something special going on?

**V-21**  Hi. I want to deposit $100 of this check to my savings account and put the rest in my checking account. Here is my checking account deposit already made out; but I'm not sure what my savings account number is. Can you find it? I'll be glad to make out the deposit for you if you want me to.

You've handled those transactions very well. You should be able to work alone tomorrow. It's time now for you to close your window for the day. You might want to use the information on page 66 to help with this task. Complete your Tally Sheet to simulate counting the cash in your cash drawer and balance your cash. Use the Midtown Bank software to print your Daily Account Activity report and your Cash Drawer Activity report.

In order to prepare your work area for tomorrow's activities, submit your working papers to your supervisor for evaluation.

## Unit Check Activity                                    Unit V

**Instructions:** *In the appropriate blank, write the word or phrase from the list of terms that will best complete the following sentences. When you are finished, remove and submit your completed Unit Check to your instructor for evaluation.*

### List of Terms

| | | |
|---|---|---|
| account balance | deposit | sign |
| cash activity | endorsements | stop payment order |
| Cash Drawer Activity report | making change | subtracts |
| cash on hand | on-line | tellers |
| computer cash account | Proof | Transaction Request Form |

1. When a teller disburses money to a customer, she or he _____

   that amount from the customer's account.

2. All checks being deposited should have proper _____.

3. _____ must balance cash at the end of the banking day.

4. The _____ is a teller's means of keeping track

   of money handled.

5. A(n) _____ is money put in a customer's account.

6. All banks charge a fee for a(n) _____.

7. A customer must sign a(n) _____ to get

   money from his or her savings account.

8. Balancing is a summary of all _____ for a teller's window.

9. When your cash transactions do not balance, you must enter the difference

   (less shortage/plus overage) on the _____.

**10.** A teller is said to be in balance when _____ equals

computer net cash.

**11.** A teller must verify a sufficient _____ before

cashing a check for a customer.

**12.** All deposit tickets and deposited negotiable instruments go to the

_____ department.

**13.** A customer must _____ the deposit ticket when

he or she receives some cash from the deposit.

**14.** A transaction where no computer entry at all is made is

_____

**15.** When tellers enter transactions directly to customer accounts, they are

said to be _____

# A DAY AT THE TELLER WINDOW

## Objectives

At the completion of Unit VI, you will be able to:

- Complete a day's transactions at a teller workstation (window).
- Successfully answer questions concerning your bank teller position.

# Working as a Full-Time Teller

Now that you've finished your teller training, you are being assigned to a teller window on a regular basis. At this window, you'll be accepting deposits, disbursing cash, and giving assistance and information to customers. As you learned during your training, we have special teller windows for other transactions, such

as loan payments and preparation and sale of negotiable instruments (money orders, traveler's checks, and so on). Also, our customer service representatives open new accounts and provide other banking services. We usually assign experienced employees who have demonstrated dependability and initiative to these workstations. We hope you, too, will soon qualify to progress to one of those positions.

Your activities today will be similar to those you completed while you were being observed in Unit V. Today should be a slow day so you will be able to take your time with each customer as you serve his or her needs. Refer to this *Employee Manual* or the Help menu in the Midtown Bank software if you need to review any procedures. If a customer's signature is required on any item, simulate the signing by writing the required signature; then process the item.

You have some time before the bank opens for business today to prepare your work area. You will be using the envelopes that you used in Unit V. Find the forms and working documents labeled VI in the back of the *Employee Manual* and be prepared to remove them as you need them. Have paper clips, a file folder, pen, and pencil handy for use at your workstation. Arrange these items so you can easily reach and use them as you work through the day's activities.

Note on the Tally Sheet for Unit VI that the amount of cash brought forward from the day before is entered (Section 2). This represents the cash that is in your drawer at the beginning of each day ($5,000). All cash over this amount from the previous day's business has been transferred to the bank's vault. Keep this Tally Sheet in your work area and enter each cash transaction at the time it is made as you did in Unit V.

Now you're almost ready to open your teller window for customers. Remember to check for proper endorsements on deposited items. Also remember our check cashing policies. If you have a problem with a check you can't cash, call your supervisor for help.

As you complete each transaction, consider how you will respond to the customer—what you will say and do. Keep in mind the Human Relations Tips you have seen in this manual as you deal with your customers. If you have a customer with an unusual request or problem, make a note of your action so you can discuss it later with your supervisor. Use the space just below the dialogue for these notes or any other notes about the transaction.

The proof department, of course, will check all the transactions you make, but it is still very important for you to do your work accurately. With the number of customers you'll have today, it might be difficult to trace an error at the end of the day. Speaking of customers, the doors are about to open. Good luck!

# Work Assignment

**Instructions:** *Today is May 18. Continue with your time worked record. If you have not already done so, launch the Midtown Bank software and open your data file. You will be working at the lobby teller window (not the drive-thru window), so click the Teller Window hot spot and then click OK to begin working. Remember, if you accidentally access the wrong customer account, **do not** advance the bookmarking. This way, you will be able to continue with your work without any adverse effects on the rest of the transactions.*

## Job No.

**VI-1**  Good morning. Sure glad I'm first in line. I have to open up the business today and I can't be late. I need to make a deposit.

**VI-2**  Boy! I have to wait in line everywhere I go these days! If you only knew how rushed everyone is in the morning, you would open up earlier for your customers. I need to cash this check and I don't want any $1 bills.

**VI-3**  Hi! I need to keep some cash out of this deposit. Please give me a roll of dimes, a roll of nickels, and a roll of quarters for school lunches for my children.

**VI-4**  There are a number of checks in this deposit. Hope I added them correctly. By the way, can you tell me the balance in my savings account?

**VI-5**  I want to deposit my paycheck; but I need $100 cash—four twenties and two tens will be fine.

**VI-6**  Hi! I just need to cash this check.

| VI-7 | Good morning. Are you new? I don't remember seeing you before. I'd like to make a deposit. |
|---|---|
| VI-8 | Hello. Can you cash this check for me? I have an account at this bank. |
| VI-9 | I need to deposit this money. This bill looks like it has been washed or something. Would you look at it and see if it's OK? |
| VI-10 | Do I need to sign this deposit ticket? I want to get some cash from it. |
| VI-11 | Did you see her diamonds? Who was that, some celebrity? Bet she has a lot of money! |
| VI-12 | This deposit goes in my checking account. |
| VI-13 | Is it ever hot today! We just arrived home from our vacation and have some traveler's checks left. Can you believe that? I'd like to deposit them into my savings account. |
| VI-14 | Good morning. I need to cash this check. Dotty, you forgot to sign this check. I'm sure glad you came with me! |
| VI-15 | You're new, aren't you? Are you sure you know how to handle my deposit? |

---

**VI-16**    I need to cash this check for $30. I did some yard work for this guy, and
he told me he has an account at this bank. I'd like ten-dollar bills please.

---

**VI-17**    I need to withdraw some money from my savings account. What do I
need to do? I need $100 in twenties.

---

**VI-18**    Hi! When do you think this deposit will get into my checking account?
I also need you to transfer $500 from my savings to my checking. My
savings account number is 596-431-2. Do I need to sign something?

---

**VI-19**    Here's my deposit. Sorry there is so much money in coins. I've been
saving these for a long time, and I wrapped them last night so I could
deposit them in my savings account today.

---

**VI-20**    Am I in the right place to open a new checking account? I've been
noticing your sidewalk teller terminals around town, and I thought it
would be a lot more convenient for me to do my banking with you.

---

**VI-21**    I need to cash my payroll check. I have an account here. I need two
Alexander Hamiltons and twenty George Washingtons. It doesn't matter
about the rest.

---

**VI-22**    Here's my deposit. Please hurry, I'm late.

---

**VI-23**    I had a great birthday this year. It's about time I started saving for college.
Can you open a savings account for me? I have a checking account and
all the personal information would be the same. My name is Robert D.
Ramsey. My account number is 386-493-2.

**VI-24** Please cash this $100 check. I need a crisp, new $100 bill for my grandson for his birthday.

**VI-25** Hello. Can you tell me why there's a $15 charge on my checking account on May 2? I didn't write a check and I haven't ordered new checks or anything. My account number is 581-496-1.

**VI-26** I want to transfer $1,000 from my checking account to my savings account. I need to earn some interest on that money.

**VI-27** I need to cash a check. I told my children I would reward them for their good grades. Let's see, I need two fives and the rest ones.

**VI-28** I have a deposit to make. Oh, is the computer down? Does this mean you can't put this money in my account now? I hope you can put this money in my account before the day is over. My balance is pretty low.

**VI-29** The computer is down? I assume you can't tell me my balance then. That's OK. I'm just in the habit of checking it when I make my deposits.

**VI-30** Can you cash this check? My account number is 684-938-1.

**VI-31** Hello! How's it going today? Here's my deposit.

**VI-32** What would you say if I told you this is a holdup? Don't get excited. I'm just joking. I didn't realize you'd take it so seriously. I'll never do that again. Now I've almost forgotten why I'm here!

**VI-33**    I want to transfer $250 to my checking account from my savings account. My checking account number is 486-801-1, but I'm not sure what my savings account number is.

**VI-34**    I forgot this when I was here earlier. I want to deposit this in my grand-child's savings account. Her account number is 694-368-2. I've been doing this every year for the past ten years. I'm amazed how fast it adds up.

**VI-35**    We had a good afternoon at the art festival in Central Park.

**VI-36**    I need three rolls of nickels, five rolls of pennies, two rolls of dimes, and two rolls of quarters. How much do I need to make this check for?

**VI-37**    How much would I have left if I took $500 out of my savings account? It's number 421-684-6. I'm Shelly Wiemer. Oh really? Well, just transfer $200 from my savings account into my checking account. That number is 421-684-5.

**VI-38**    I signed a stop payment form on check number 282 last week. I just wanted to check on it while I'm in the bank on some other business. My account number is 861-593-2.

**VI-39**    Here's my deposit.

**VI-40**    Hello.

**VI-41**    I guess you're about ready to close. I'm sure glad you allow all the people in line to make their deposits. Thanks so much.

The bank is now closed to customers. It's time for you to complete your closing activities.

**1.** Complete your balancing activities. (Review the steps for balancing, if necessary, in Unit V or in the software Help.) Use the Tally Sheet on which you entered today's cash transactions.

**2.** Complete your other closing activities and submit all items used in the closing activities and all items in your Proof Department/Supervisor envelope to your supervisor. Remember to print the Daily Account Activity and Cash Drawer Activity reports. Sign your name on each report and submit them with the other materials to your supervisor.

You are now ready to prepare for the final examination. You may want to review the *Employee Manual* before you complete this examination. When you are ready, ask your supervisor for the examination. Complete the exam as directed and submit it to your supervisor.

Now that you are finished with your work at Midtown Bank, you deserve a paycheck. Follow these steps to get paid:

**1.** Go to the Midtown Bank lobby and click the Payroll Department hot spot.

**2.** Carefully read the dialog box that appears on your screen. Make sure you are completely finished with all of your work. Once you have printed a paycheck, you cannot print it again. If you are sure you are finished with the simulation, click Yes. Otherwise, click No so you can finish your work.

**3.** A paycheck appears on your screen. Print the paycheck by pulling down the File menu, choosing the Print command, and then clicking OK.

**4.** Save your file and exit the simulation.

Remove your timecard from the *Employee Manual*, complete it, and submit to your supervisor.

Congratulations! You are now a full-time teller at Midtown Bank. The training you have experienced has given you skills and insight that should help you in any future teller or cashiering position and in daily business transactions with others.

# APPENDIX A
# USING THE
# MIDTOWN BANK
# SOFTWARE

The Midtown Bank software is very easy to use. Pull-down menus and icons (pictures that represent software functions) allow you to access the various features of the software. As you work through the simulation, you can use this appendix as a quick reference for descriptions of the menus and icons.

If you are using a Macintosh computer, your screen may look slightly different than the illustrations shown in this *Employee Manual*. Rest assured that you will be able to follow the instructions provided, even though your screen may not always look exactly the same.

## ■ Using the Pull-Down Menus

The Midtown Bank menu bar, shown in Figure A.1, contains six menu options: File, Accounts, Reports, Seminars, Options, and Help. During your teller training, you will be asked to pull down a specific menu and choose one of the commands. **Commands** are the choices listed when a menu is pulled down. Sometimes, an option on the menu bar or some commands on a pull-down menu may be dimmed. This means the option or command is not available for use at that particular time.

| File | Accounts | Reports | Seminars | Options | Help |

**Figure A.1**

*Midtown Bank Menu Bar*

The way you pull down menus and choose commands varies slightly according to the type of computer you are using.

### USING AN IBM PC OR COMPATIBLE COMPUTER

If you are using an IBM PC or compatible computer, you can pull down a menu in one of two ways:

1. You can use the mouse to point the arrow pointer at the menu you wish to pull down. When the arrow is positioned over the menu, click the left mouse button one time. The menu will drop down, allowing you to see the commands available.

**2.** You can press ALT in conjunction with the underlined letter for the menu option. For example, to pull down the File menu, you would hold down ALT and then press F.

To choose a command from a menu, you would usually use the mouse to click the command you wish to use. However, you can also press the underlined letter to choose the command. So, to choose Exit from the File menu, you can press X while the File menu is pulled down.

The Midtown Bank software also includes some built-in **speed keys** that let you choose commands without pulling down the menu first. To use a speed key, press the control key (shown as **Ctrl** on the menu and on some keyboards) along with a specified key to activate the command. For example, to exit the Midtown Bank software, you can use the **Ctrl+X** speed key. Not all menu commands have speed keys. When a speed key is available, it is shown to the right of the command on the pull-down menu. As the various menus are discussed in the following sections of this appendix, the speed keys are indicated when they are available.

### USING A MACINTOSH COMPUTER

If you are using a Macintosh computer, use the mouse to position the pointer arrow over the menu option you wish to use. Press the mouse button to pull down the menu. The menu will drop down, allowing you to see the commands available. To choose a command, roll the mouse until the command you want to use is highlighted, and then release the mouse button. Note that as soon as you release the mouse button the menu will close, so you need to keep the mouse button pressed until the command you want to use is highlighted.

The Midtown Bank software also includes some built-in **speed keys** that let you choose commands without pulling down the menu first. To use a speed key, press the command key (shown as ⌘) along with a specified key to activate the command. For example, to quit the Midtown Bank software, you can use the ⌘-**Q** speed key. Not all menu commands have speed keys. When a speed key is available, it is shown to the right of the command on the pull-down menu. As the various menus are discussed in the following sections of this appendix, the speed keys are indicated when they are available.

As you use the Midtown Bank software, you will often be asked to key information and then press ENTER. When using a Macintosh computer, you should press RETURN whenever you are asked to press ENTER.

# ■ Touring the Menus

During your training, you will use the menus and commands in the Midtown Bank software to complete your daily activities. This section provides a brief description of the commands available in each of the menus. Speed keys are also indicated when they are available. Remember, IBM PC speed keys are preceded with **Ctrl**, and Macintosh speed keys are preceded with ⌘. So, if you see a speed key of ⌘-**Q**, you can use it only on a Macintosh computer. If you see a speed key of **Ctrl+X**, you can use it only on an IBM PC or compatible computer.

In most cases, the IBM PC and Macintosh versions of the software work in exactly the same way. Differences between the software versions are identified as they occur.

## THE FILE MENU

The commands in the File menu (Figure A.2) are used to perform file operations, such as saving files, closing files, and exiting the software.

- **New (⌘-N).** You only use the New command when you first begin the simulation, or if for some reason you need to start again from the very beginning. When you choose the New command, you will be asked to provide your name, your teacher's name, and a password. The Midtown Bank software will also generate an Employee Log that is updated each time you use the software. The log keeps track of how many hours you spend working for the bank. Be very careful when using the New command. If you choose this command after you have already started using the software, all work completed to date (except your log-in information and your password) will be erased!

- **Open (⌘-O).** You use the Open command to open your existing data files. After you have started the simulation, you will probably need to stop periodically and pick up your work the next day. The Open command lets you start working where you left off the last time. The Employee Log keeps track of when you open your data files so that you can be paid for the hours you have worked.

**Figure A.2**

*The File Menu*

- **Close (Ctrl+C, ⌘-W).** The Close command closes your data files, but still leaves the Midtown Bank software running so another student can use it. You should always close your data files when you are finished working; otherwise, another student could accidentally use your work. The Close command also updates your Employee Log to include the amount of time you worked for the day.

- **Save (Ctrl+S, ⌘-S).** Use the Save command to save your work. In addition to saving your files at the end of each work session, you should save your files frequently *during* each work session. This way, you won't lose data if the power goes out or some other catastrophe occurs.

- **Print Setup/Page Setup.** You use this command to tell the Midtown Bank software about your printer. You probably will not need to use the Print Setup/Page Setup command because the Midtown Bank software is designed to work with most printers. If you try to print a report and have difficulty doing so, you may need help from your supervisor to set up the software for your printer.

- **Print (⌘-P).** You use the Print command to print the information currently displayed on your screen. This command will be used when it is time to print your paycheck.

- **Exit/Quit (Ctrl+X, ⌘-Q).** You use the Exit/Quit command to quit the simulation.

## THE ACCOUNTS MENU

The commands in the Accounts menu (Figure A.3) let you work with customer accounts, the cash drawer, and the vault.

**Figure A.3**

*The Accounts Menu*

- **Customer (⌘-U).** The Customer command opens the Customer Account Access window. This window is a list of the names and corresponding numbers of customer accounts. By default, customer accounts are listed in alphabetical order by last name. You can change the display order to numerical by clicking the Setup button on the right side of the Customer Account Access window and then choosing Numerical. After you have opened a specific customer account, you can find such information as the current balance in the account, the address of the owner(s), and so on. The Customer command is not available unless you are at a teller window.

- **Cash Drawer (⌘-H).** The Cash Drawer command opens the Cash Drawer Account window. This window shows all cash transactions made during the day. For example, if a customer cashes a check, you will transfer money from your cash drawer to the customer. The transaction will be reflected in the Cash Drawer Account, making it easy to see the transfer of cash that takes place during the day. If your cash drawer is out of balance at the end of the day, you can use the Cash Drawer command to see all the transactions that took place and make corrections to the transactions if necessary. The Cash Drawer command is not available unless the cash drawer is unlocked.

- **Vault.** Midtown Bank does not want you to keep excess cash in your cash drawer, so you should transfer any cash over $7,000 from your cash drawer to the vault any time during the banking day. You use the Vault command to transfer this excess cash.

## THE REPORTS MENU

The Reports menu (Figure A.4) is used to print reports of daily account activity and cash drawer activity. You will need to print these reports at the end of each day, but you can also print them at any time if you want to check account or cash drawer activity.

**Figure A.4**

*The Reports Menu*

- **Daily Account Activity.** The Daily Account Activity report is a list of all the transactions you processed during the day. This report provides an audit trail of work completed and helps you trace any errors.

- **Cash Drawer Activity.** The Cash Drawer Activity report is a list of your cash drawer transactions. This report is similar to the information you see when you choose the Cash Drawer command from the Accounts menu, except that you cannot make changes to the data in the report. If you see a mistake in the report, go to the Cash Drawer Account window and correct the mistake before you print your final report.

## THE SEMINARS MENU

The Seminars menu (Figure A.5) provides opportunities to learn more about the banking industry and to practice using the numeric keypad.

**Figure A.5**

*The Seminars Menu*

- **Keypad Workshop.** The Keypad Workshop provides practice with the numeric keypad. The software supplies feedback about your accuracy so you can monitor your progress.

- **Counterfeit Currency and Money Facts.** All bank tellers must be able to distinguish between counterfeit currency and U.S. legal tender. The Midtown Bank software provides this seminar to help you identify counterfeit bills.

- **Security and Emergency Procedures.** This seminar describes Midtown Bank's policies in the event of an emergency. Would you know what to do if someone tries to steal the money from your cash drawer? What should you do if you see a suspicious-looking person in the bank? This seminar explains how to protect yourself and the bank's customers in the event of an emergency.

## THE OPTIONS MENU

The Options menu (Figure A.6) provides a variety of tools, such as a numeric keypad, to assist you as you complete the day's activities.

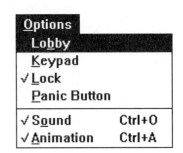

**Figure A.6**

*The Options Menu*

- **Lobby (⌘-B).** You use the Lobby command to access the teller and drive-thru windows, receive feedback from your supervisor, interact with customer service representatives, and collect your paycheck. To activate a section of the lobby, click it with the mouse. For example, to access the drive-thru window, click the desk in front of the window. You will use the Lobby command to move around the bank as you complete your daily activities.

- **Keypad (⌘-K).** Use the Keypad command to display an on-screen numeric keypad. The numbers you key will appear on the screen. You can use the keypad to verify totals on deposit tickets or to balance your cash drawer.

- **Lock (⌘-L).** The Lock command locks and unlocks the cash drawer. It is a *toggle* command—choosing it the first time unlocks the cash drawer, choosing it a second time locks the cash drawer. You will need to unlock the drawer at the start of each workday, and you should lock the drawer each time you leave the teller window. A check mark next to the Lock command means the cash drawer is locked.

- **Panic Button.** The Panic Button is used only in emergency situations, such as during a robbery. If you use the Panic Button inappropriately, you will be asked to repeat the Security and Emergency Procedures seminar.

- **Sound (Ctrl+O).** The Sound command turns on and off the sounds generated by the Midtown Bank software. It is a toggle command—choosing it the first time turns the sound off, choosing it a second time turns the sound back on. A check mark next to the Sound command means the sound is turned on.

- **Animation (Ctrl+A).** The Animation command turns on and off the animation in the Midtown Bank software. If you are using an older computer, the animation may cause the Midtown Bank software to run a little more slowly than you might like. Turning off the animation can help speed up the software. The Animation command is a toggle command—choosing it the first time turns the animation off, choosing it a second time turns the animation back on. A check mark next to the Animation command means the animation is turned on.

## THE HELP MENU

Although the Midtown Bank software is easy to use, you may find you need help with a particular feature. If this happens, you can use the commands available in the Help menu (Figure A.7).

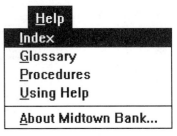

**Figure A.7**

*The Help Menu*

- **Index.** The Index command provides an index of the help topics available. Choose Index from the Help menu and key the name of the software feature with which you need help.

- **Glossary.** The Glossary is a list of common bank terms and their definitions.

- **Procedures.** This command provides on-line information for specific teller procedures described in the *Employee Manual.*

- **Using Help.** Choose this command if you need to learn more about using the Help system.

- **About Midtown Bank.** This command provides information about the Midtown Bank software, such as the version number of the software and the year it was developed. Macintosh users will access the About Midtown Bank command from the Apple menu.

# Using Icons

You will use some features of the Midtown Bank software with almost every transaction; you will use other features only one or two times. So you can easily access those features that you need on a regular basis, a series of **icons** (pictures) is provided beneath the menu bar and Message box of the Midtown Bank software.

To access the command represented by the icon, just use the mouse to click the icon. You do not need to worry about pulling down menus or using speed keys. Sometimes an icon may be dimmed. This means the command is not available for use at that particular time.

 **Lobby.** Clicking the Lobby icon has the same effect as choosing the Lobby command from the Options menu.

 **Close.** The Close icon lets you close the scenario. It has the same effect as choosing the Close command from the File menu.

 **Save.** The Save icon saves the scenario. It has the same effect as choosing the Save command from the File menu.

 **Exit.** The Exit icon lets you exit the program. It has the same effect as choosing the Exit command from the File menu.

 **Customer Accounts.** The Customer Accounts icon opens the Customer Accounts Access window. It has the same effect as choosing Customer from the Accounts menu.

 **Lock.** The Lock icon lets you lock or unlock the cash drawer. It has the same effect as choosing Lock from the Options menu.

 **Cash Drawer.** The Cash Drawer icon has the same effect as choosing Cash Drawer from the Accounts menu. The Cash Drawer icon is not available unless the cash drawer is unlocked.

 **Vault.** The Vault icon has the same effect as choosing Vault from the Accounts menu.

 **Keypad.** Clicking on the Keypad icon displays the numeric keypad. This icon has the same effect as choosing Keypad from the Options menu.

 **Help-Index.** The Help-Index icon lets you access the list of banking topics available in the on-line Help system. It has the same effect as choosing the Index command from the Help menu.

# Other Features of the Midtown Bank Software

In addition to the pull-down menus and icons, the Midtown Bank software has some additional features to help you train as a bank teller.

## BANK LOBBY HOT SPOTS

The Bank Lobby window has several "hot spots" that are activated when clicked with the mouse (Figure A.8). These hot spots allow you to move quickly to different areas of the lobby. You can find the hot spots easily because the mouse arrow becomes a pointing finger when on a hot spot.

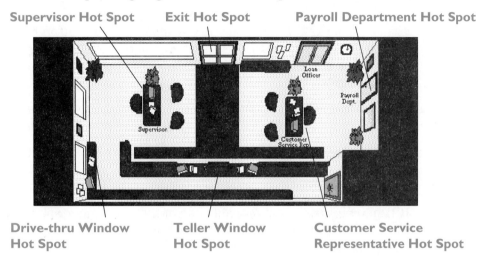

Supervisor Hot Spot     Exit Hot Spot     Payroll Department Hot Spot

Drive-thru Window Hot Spot     Teller Window Hot Spot     Customer Service Representative Hot Spot

**Figure A.8**

*Hot Spots in the Bank Lobby*

- **Drive-thru Window.** When you click the desk at the Drive-thru window, you will "zoom in" on this section of the bank (Figure A.9). Within the Drive-thru window, the cash drawer lock and panic button are additional hot spots. Clicking the cash drawer lock hot spot locks and unlocks the cash drawer. Clicking the panic button hot spot signals the bank's security department that an emergency is taking place.

  You must be at either the Drive-thru window or the Teller window to access customer accounts and complete transactions. You will work at the Drive-thru window while you complete Units I-V of the *Employee Manual*.

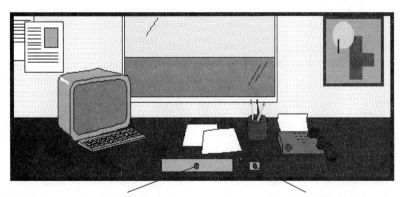

Cash Drawer Lock Hot Spot     Panic Button Hot Spot

**Figure A.9**

*The Drive-Thru Window*

- **Teller Window.** When you click the Teller window, you will "zoom in" on this area of the lobby and be able to process transactions for walk-in customers. (See Figure A.10.) Within the Teller window, the cash drawer lock and panic button are additional hot spots. Clicking the cash drawer lock hot

**Figure A.10**

*The Teller Window*

**Cash Drawer Lock Hot Spot**          **Panic Button Hot Spot**

spot locks and unlocks the cash drawer. Clicking the panic button hot spot signals the bank's security department that an emergency is taking place.

You will work at the Teller window while you complete Unit VI of the *Employee Manual*.

- **Supervisor's Desk.** Click the hot spot at the supervisor's desk to receive information or to notify your supervisor of a possible security problem.

- **Customer Service Representative's Desk.** Click the hot spot at the customer service representative's desk when a customer wants to open a new account or has a request that cannot be handled at the teller window.

- **Payroll Department.** This is probably one of the most important hot spots on the screen—click the payroll department hot spot to receive your paycheck. Make sure you are completely finished with the simulation before printing your paycheck. Once a paycheck is printed, your file is closed. If you find a mistake in a simulation transaction after the check is printed, you cannot correct it and you would need to start the simulation over again from the beginning. You may view your paycheck without printing it as many times as you wish.

## POP-UP QUESTIONS

Since the goal of this simulation is to help you learn many of the skills you would need as a bank teller, pop-up questions are built into the Midtown Bank software to quiz you on topics presented in the *Employee Manual* and the seminars. (These questions will not appear until you work on the transactions in Unit VI.) For example, you might be asked how to handle a particular emergency situation based on information from the software seminars. The instructions on the screen will tell you where to key your answer and how to exit the pop-up question. Some of the questions have a time limit, so you should always answer as quickly and accurately as you can. You never know when one of these questions might pop up, so be sure to read the information in your *Employee Manual* before using the software!

## EMERGENCY SITUATIONS AND INTERRUPTIONS

As in any business, workdays at Midtown Bank are often filled with interruptions. You may be interrupted by a fax or some sort of emergency. You will learn how to respond to these emergencies as you complete your bank teller training. Make sure you know how to handle these situations so you can respond appropriately when the time comes.

Now that you are familiar with the Midtown Bank software, it's time to get to work. We hope you enjoy working at Midtown Bank!

# APPENDIX B
# LAUNCHING THE MIDTOWN BANK SOFTWARE

The Midtown Bank software is available for Macintosh and IBM PC or compatible computers. This appendix explains how to launch the Midtown Bank software on your computer, assuming the software has already been installed. If the software has not been installed, check with your instructor before continuing.

To launch the Midtown Bank software, follow the instructions for the type of computer you are using. **Note:** These instructions assume you are using a stand-alone computer system. If you are using a network, your instructor can tell you how to launch the software.

## ■ Launching the Software on an IBM PC or Compatible Computer

Follow these steps to launch the Midtown Bank software on an IBM PC or compatible computer:

1. Turn on your computer and monitor.

2. In order to use the Midtown Bank software, your computer must be running Microsoft® Windows®[1]. If Windows is not automatically launched when you turn on your computer, launch it now. If you are not sure how to launch Windows, check with your instructor before continuing.

3. Access the Midtown Bank Simulation and find the Midtown Bank icon.

4. Double-click the Midtown Bank icon to launch the Midtown Bank software. The Midtown Bank opening screen will appear. The opening screen sound and animation can be stopped by pressing any key.

   You are now ready to use the Midtown Bank software.

[1]Microsoft and Windows are registered trademarks of Microsoft Corporation.

# Launching the Software on a Macintosh Computer

Follow these steps to launch the Midtown Bank software on a Macintosh computer:

1. Turn on your computer. (If your computer has a separate monitor, be sure to turn it on, too.)

2. Open the Midtown Bank folder and find the Midtown Bank icon.

3. Double-click the Midtown Bank icon to launch the Midtown Bank software. The Midtown Bank opening screen will appear. The opening screen sound and animation can be stopped by pressing any key.

You are now ready to use the Midtown Bank software.

# TIME WORKED RECORD

NAME _____

SOC. SEC. NO. _____

| DAY | DATE | TIME IN | TIME OUT | TOTAL HRS. |
|-----|------|---------|----------|------------|
| Monday | | | | |
| Tuesday | | | | |
| Wednesday | | | | |
| Thursday | | | | |
| Friday | | | | |

WEEKLY TOTAL _____

| DAY | DATE | TIME IN | TIME OUT | TOTAL HRS. |
|-----|------|---------|----------|------------|
| Monday | | | | |
| Tuesday | | | | |
| Wednesday | | | | |
| Thursday | | | | |
| Friday | | | | |

WEEKLY TOTAL _____

| DAY | DATE | TIME IN | TIME OUT | TOTAL HRS. |
|-----|------|---------|----------|------------|
| Monday | | | | |
| Tuesday | | | | |
| Wednesday | | | | |
| Thursday | | | | |
| Friday | | | | |

WEEKLY TOTAL _____

| DAY | DATE | TIME IN | TIME OUT | TOTAL HRS. |
|-----|------|---------|----------|------------|
| Monday | | | | |
| Tuesday | | | | |
| Wednesday | | | | |
| Thursday | | | | |
| Friday | | | | |

WEEKLY TOTAL _____

TOTAL HRS. THIS TIMECARD _____

Employee's Signature _____

Supervisor's Signature _____

## Check 2715 (III-1)

**GEORGE T. LUCAS, ESQ.**
708 PARK LANE
DALLAS, TX 75223

32-2/1110

May 13, 19 --

PAY TO THE ORDER OF _Penny Department Store_   $ 189.43

One hundred eighty-nine and 43/100 —————————— DOLLARS

**Midtown Bank**
Dallas, Texas

FOR _shoes_   _George T. Lucas, Esq._

FOR CLASSROOM USE ONLY

⑈110000 20⑈ 2715⑈ 38695 2⑈

## Check 5654 (III-2)

**UNDERHILL ANIMAL CLINIC**
514 SYCAMORE DRIVE
DALLAS, TX 75148

32-2/1110

May 2, 19 --

PAY TO THE ORDER OF _Pugg Supply Company_   $ 821.76

Eight hundred twenty-one and 76/100 —————— DOLLARS

**Midtown Bank**
Dallas, Texas

FOR _Inv. 3899.67_   _Kirk E. Kohler_

FOR CLASSROOM USE ONLY

⑈110000 20⑈ 5654⑈ 50635⑈

## Check 8233 (III-3)

**DALE F. OR MONICA L. SHARP**
1408 TURTLE CREEK BLVD.
DALLAS, TX 75219

32-2/1110

May 1, 19 --

PAY TO THE ORDER OF _University Savings Assoc._   $ 650.00

Six hundred fifty and no/100 ———————————— DOLLARS

**Midtown Bank**
Dallas, Texas

FOR _Loan 1099-4C_   _Monica L. Sharp_

FOR CLASSROOM USE ONLY

⑈110000 20⑈ 8233⑈ 48379 25⑈

## Check 0700 (III-4)

**THOMAS J. JONES OR DANIEL W. JONES**
3216 CARLISLE ST.
DALLAS, TX 75204

32-2/1110

May 8, 19 __

PAY TO THE ORDER OF _Jill Jones_   $ 50.00

Fifty and no/100 ——————————————— DOLLARS

**Midtown Bank**
Dallas, Texas

FOR _HAPPY BIRTHDAY_   _Daniel W. Jones_

FOR CLASSROOM USE ONLY

⑈110000 20⑈ 0700 59168 2⑈

## Check 12647 (III-5)

**FLACK ELECTRONICS**
5719 LIVE OAK AVENUE
DALLAS, TX 75206

32-2/1110

May 2, 19 --

PAY TO THE ORDER OF _Jonathan Holmes, Inc._   $ 1,643.56

One thousand six hundred forty-three 56/100 DOLLARS

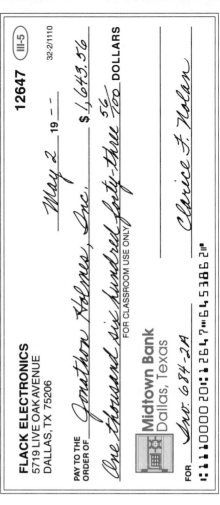

**Midtown Bank**
Dallas, Texas

FOR _Inv. 684-2A_   _Clarice F. Nolan_

FOR CLASSROOM USE ONLY

⑈110000 20⑈ 12647⑈ 64 5386 2⑈

## Check 1224 (III-6)

**LELLA S. PETROSINA**
1964 CRESTVIEW DR.
DALLAS, TX 75154

32-2/1110

May 13, 19 --

PAY TO THE ORDER OF _Sybil's Salon_   $ 24.62

Twenty-four and 62/100 ——————————— DOLLARS

**Midtown Bank**
Dallas, Texas

FOR _hair products_   _Lella S. Petrosina_

FOR CLASSROOM USE ONLY

⑈110000 20⑈ 1224⑈ 68348 15⑈

## Check III-7 (No. 0412)

**KENNETH R. TITUS**
527 SATURN ROAD
GARLAND, TX 75002

32-2/1110

May 6 19 —

PAY TO THE ORDER OF _A-Plus Office Supplies_ $ 246.98

_Two hundred forty-six and 89/100_ DOLLARS

**Midtown Bank**
Dallas, Texas

FOR CLASSROOM USE ONLY

FOR _Supplies_

Kenneth R. Titus

⑈⑆110000 20⑆0412⑆68349⑈

---

## Check III-8 (No. 0209)

**A. C. OR NICOLE A. YOAKUM**
7205 BRIGHTON
DALLAS, TX 75208

32-2/1110

May 6 19 —

PAY TO THE ORDER OF _Kelly-Jones Oil Co._ $ 38.49

_Thirty-eight and 49/100_ DOLLARS

**Midtown Bank**
Dallas, Texas

FOR CLASSROOM USE ONLY

FOR _Acct. 694-271-3_

Nicole A. Yoakum

⑈⑆110000 20⑆0209⑆68395⑈

---

## Check III-9 (No. 1654)

**A. R. TURNER-CARR**
1534 MARSHALL DRIVE
DALLAS, TX 75240

32-2/1110

May 7 19 —

PAY TO THE ORDER OF _Montgomery Realtors_ $ 475.00

_Four hundred seventy-five and no/100_ DOLLARS

**Midtown Bank**
Dallas, Texas

FOR CLASSROOM USE ONLY

FOR _Rent_

Anthony Turner-Carr

⑈⑆110000 20⑆1654⑆68493 25⑈

---

## Check III-10 (No. 21582)

**ANDERSON BRICK PRODUCTS, INC.**
7122 GLENCOE
DALLAS, TX 75206

32-2/1110

May 12 19 —

PAY TO THE ORDER OF _Patricia S. Cox_ $ 543.11

_Five hundred forty-three and 11/100_ DOLLARS

**Midtown Bank**
Dallas, Texas

FOR CLASSROOM USE ONLY

FOR _Expenses_

Martha S. Anderson
PRESIDENT
VICE PRESIDENT

⑈⑆110000 20⑆2158⑆68794 35⑈

---

## Check III-11 (No. 0292)

**JANIS B. WALL**
7215 RIDGECREST DR.
DALLAS, TX 75231

32-2/1110

May 13 19 —

PAY TO THE ORDER OF _Walter O'Malley_ $ 11.98

_Twenty-seven and 98/100_ DOLLARS

**Midtown Bank**
Dallas, Texas

FOR CLASSROOM USE ONLY

FOR _Bal. due_

Janis B. Wall

⑈⑆110000 20⑆0292⑆691086 5⑈

---

## Check III-12 (No. 0896)

**MR. OR MRS. ALFRED C. DARROW**
9433 BASELINE DR.
DALLAS, TX 75243

32-2/1110

April 20 19 —

PAY TO THE ORDER OF _O'Reilly's_ $ 28.75

_Twenty-eight and 75/100_ DOLLARS

**Midtown Bank**
Dallas, Texas

FOR CLASSROOM USE ONLY

FOR

Alfred C. Darrow

⑈⑆110000 20⑆0896⑆86349 2⑈

**ENDORSE HERE**

A-Plus Office Supplies
acct 6945732

**DO NOT WRITE, STAMP OR SIGN BELOW THIS LINE**
RESERVED FOR FINANCIAL INSTITUTION USE*

*FEDERAL RESERVE BOARD OF GOVERNORS REG. CC

**ENDORSE HERE**

Kelly Jones Oil Co.
For Deposit only

**DO NOT WRITE, STAMP OR SIGN BELOW THIS LINE**
RESERVED FOR FINANCIAL INSTITUTION USE*

*FEDERAL RESERVE BOARD OF GOVERNORS REG. CC

**ENDORSE HERE**

For deposit only
Montgomery Realtors
acct. 6942496

**DO NOT WRITE, STAMP OR SIGN BELOW THIS LINE**
RESERVED FOR FINANCIAL INSTITUTION USE*

*FEDERAL RESERVE BOARD OF GOVERNORS REG. CC

**ENDORSE HERE**

Patricia Cox

**DO NOT WRITE, STAMP OR SIGN BELOW THIS LINE**
RESERVED FOR FINANCIAL INSTITUTION USE*

*FEDERAL RESERVE BOARD OF GOVERNORS REG. CC

**ENDORSE HERE**

For deposit
Walter O'Malley

**DO NOT WRITE, STAMP OR SIGN BELOW THIS LINE**
RESERVED FOR FINANCIAL INSTITUTION USE*

*FEDERAL RESERVE BOARD OF GOVERNORS REG. CC

**ENDORSE HERE**

O'Reilly's
acct. 261-483-5

**DO NOT WRITE, STAMP OR SIGN BELOW THIS LINE**
RESERVED FOR FINANCIAL INSTITUTION USE*

*FEDERAL RESERVE BOARD OF GOVERNORS REG. CC

**0873** III-16

GREGORY S. AND JOYCE A. BRUCKER
5627 HIGHLAND OAKS
DALLAS, TX 75232

32-2/1110

May 1 19 --

PAY TO THE ORDER OF _Gody's Pizza_ $ 26 78

Twenty-six and 78/100 _____ DOLLARS

FOR CLASSROOM USE ONLY

Midtown Bank
Dallas, Texas

FOR _Class party_

Joyce A. Brucker
Gregory S. Brucker

⑈1110000 20⑈0873⑈34958⑈96⑈

---

**9900** III-17

GOBLE AND DOUGLAS
1681 ARAPAHO ROAD
RICHARDSON, TEXAS 75080

32-2/1110

May 9 19 --

PAY TO THE ORDER OF _City Print Shop_ $ 491.49

Four hundred ninety-one and 49/100 _____ DOLLARS

FOR CLASSROOM USE ONLY

Midtown Bank
Dallas, Texas

FOR _Balance Due_

Claude G. Goble
William R. Douglas

⑈1110000 20⑈9900⑈86254⑈⑈

---

**2191** III-18

KELLY OR JACK C. MORGAN
2503 LARAMIE DRIVE
DALLAS, TX 75149

32-2/1110

May 22 19 --

PAY TO THE ORDER OF _Tuesday Quilt Club_ $ 20.00

Twenty and 00/100 _____ DOLLARS

FOR CLASSROOM USE ONLY

Midtown Bank
Dallas, Texas

FOR _Dues_

Kelly Morgan

⑈1110000 20⑈2191⑈306452⑈⑈

---

**1113** III-13

HOLLY C. OR LOUIS CONLEY
840 WOODWARD CIRCLE
DALLAS, TX 75287

32-2/1110

May 13 19 --

PAY TO THE ORDER OF _Ronson Clothiers_ $ 169.52

One hundred sixty-nine and 52/100 _____ DOLLARS

FOR CLASSROOM USE ONLY

Midtown Bank
Dallas, Texas

FOR _Sports coats_

Louis Conley

⑈1110000 20⑈1113⑈89346⑈2⑈

---

**8646** III-14

CARLOS M. OR VERONICA VIVIANO
9995 RED BUD DRIVE
DALLAS, TX 75115

32-2/1110

May 12 19 --

PAY TO THE ORDER OF _Dodd Pharmacy_ $ 37.21

Thirty-seven and 21/100 _____ DOLLARS

FOR CLASSROOM USE ONLY

Midtown Bank
Dallas, Texas

FOR _RX64821_

Veronica Viviano

⑈1110000 20⑈8646⑈90864⑈35⑈

---

**0840** III-15

PATRICK F. OR FRANCES E. O' SULLIVAN
13123 CLEARCREST DR.
DALLAS, TX 75002

32-2/1110

May 5 19 --

PAY TO THE ORDER OF _Justin Cochran_ $ 123.11

One hundred twenty-three and 11/100 _____ DOLLARS

FOR CLASSROOM USE ONLY

Midtown Bank
Dallas, Texas

FOR _Inv. 16083_

Patrick F. O'Sullivan

⑈1110000 20⑈0840⑈58639⑈2⑈

**ENDORSE HERE**

DO NOT WRITE, STAMP OR SIGN BELOW THIS LINE
RESERVED FOR FINANCIAL INSTITUTION USE*

*FEDERAL RESERVE BOARD OF GOVERNORS REG. CC

**ENDORSE HERE**

For Deposit
Dodd Pharmacy

DO NOT WRITE, STAMP OR SIGN BELOW THIS LINE
RESERVED FOR FINANCIAL INSTITUTION USE*

*FEDERAL RESERVE BOARD OF GOVERNORS REG. CC

**ENDORSE HERE**

Jason Cochran

DO NOT WRITE, STAMP OR SIGN BELOW THIS LINE
RESERVED FOR FINANCIAL INSTITUTION USE*

*FEDERAL RESERVE BOARD OF GOVERNORS REG. CC

**ENDORSE HERE**

Jody's Pizza
for deposit

DO NOT WRITE, STAMP OR SIGN BELOW THIS LINE
RESERVED FOR FINANCIAL INSTITUTION USE*

*FEDERAL RESERVE BOARD OF GOVERNORS REG. CC

**ENDORSE HERE**

City Print Shop
For Deposit

DO NOT WRITE, STAMP OR SIGN BELOW THIS LINE
RESERVED FOR FINANCIAL INSTITUTION USE*

*FEDERAL RESERVE BOARD OF GOVERNORS REG. CC

**ENDORSE HERE**

Tuesday Quilt Club
For deposit only

DO NOT WRITE, STAMP OR SIGN BELOW THIS LINE
RESERVED FOR FINANCIAL INSTITUTION USE*

*FEDERAL RESERVE BOARD OF GOVERNORS REG. CC

# III-19

**MAURICIO I. ALVAREZ**
2514 HANOVER ST.
DALLAS, TX 75240

DATE ___May 17___ 19 __

SIGN HERE FOR LESS CASH RECEIVED

**Midtown Bank**
Dallas, Texas

⑈ ⑆1⑆10000 20⑆    ⑆⑆396501 3⑈

32-2/1110

**DEPOSIT TICKET**
USE OTHER SIDE FOR ADDITIONAL LISTING

BE SURE EACH ITEM IS PROPERLY ENDORSED

| C A S H | CURRENCY | | |
|---|---|---|---|
| | COIN | 38 | 00 |
| CHECKS (LIST SINGLY) 41-643 | | 2,861 | 00 |
| 56-793 | | 155 | 46 |
| TOTAL from reverse side | | | |
| **TOTAL** | | | |
| LESS CASH RECEIVED | | | |
| **NET DEPOSIT** | | 3,054 | 46 |

FOR CLASSROOM USE ONLY

---

# III-20

**CASEY'S CREATIONS**
18691 INDUSTRIAL, SUITE 2A
DALLAS, TX 75205

DATE ___May 17___ 19 __

SIGN HERE FOR LESS CASH RECEIVED

**Midtown Bank**
Dallas, Texas

⑈ ⑆1⑆10000 20⑆    ⑆⑆496587 8⑈

32-2/1110

**DEPOSIT TICKET**
USE OTHER SIDE FOR ADDITIONAL LISTING

BE SURE EACH ITEM IS PROPERLY ENDORSED

| C A S H | CURRENCY | | |
|---|---|---|---|
| | COIN | 500 | — |
| | | | — |
| CHECKS (LIST SINGLY) 8042 | | 10,250 | — |
| 619 | | 1,185 | 29 |
| 48956 | | 204 | 96 |
| TOTAL from reverse side | | | |
| **TOTAL** | | | |
| LESS CASH RECEIVED | | | |
| **NET DEPOSIT** | | 12,140 | 25 |

FOR CLASSROOM USE ONLY

---

# III-21

**GORDON EYE ASSOCIATES**
9865 FOREST LANE
DALLAS, TX 75230

DATE ___May 17___ 19 __

SIGN HERE FOR LESS CASH RECEIVED

**Midtown Bank**
Dallas, Texas

⑈ ⑆1⑆10000 20⑆    ⑆⑆891697 3⑈

32-2/1110

**DEPOSIT TICKET**
USE OTHER SIDE FOR ADDITIONAL LISTING

BE SURE EACH ITEM IS PROPERLY ENDORSED

| C A S H | CURRENCY | | |
|---|---|---|---|
| | COIN | 8,490 | — |
| | | 29 | — |
| CHECKS (LIST SINGLY) 10765 | | 531 | 68 |
| 08912 | | 295 | — |
| 184693 | | 1,100 | — |
| TOTAL from reverse side | | | |
| **TOTAL** | | | |
| LESS CASH RECEIVED | | | |
| **NET DEPOSIT** | | 10,435 | 68 |

FOR CLASSROOM USE ONLY

---

# III-22

**ALBERTO J. OR**
**GEORGINA L. GUERRERO**
412 BOWSER
DALLAS, TX 75219

DATE ___May 17___ 19 __

_Georgina L. Guerrero_
SIGN HERE FOR LESS CASH RECEIVED

**Midtown Bank**
Dallas, Texas

⑈ ⑆1⑆10000 20⑆    ⑆⑆469583 2⑈

32-2/1110

**DEPOSIT TICKET**
USE OTHER SIDE FOR ADDITIONAL LISTING

BE SURE EACH ITEM IS PROPERLY ENDORSED

| C A S H | CURRENCY | | |
|---|---|---|---|
| | COIN | | |
| CHECKS (LIST SINGLY) Denton | | 1,684 | 63 |
| Dallas | | 3,872 | 59 |
| TOTAL from reverse side | | | |
| **TOTAL** | | 5,557 | 22 |
| LESS CASH RECEIVED | | 250 | 00 |
| **NET DEPOSIT** | | 5,307 | 22 |

FOR CLASSROOM USE ONLY

---

# III-23

**JESSICA F. HOUSTON**
1503 COLORADO BLVD.
DALLAS, TX 75208

DATE ___May 17___ 19 __

SIGN HERE FOR LESS CASH RECEIVED

**Midtown Bank**
Dallas, Texas

⑈ ⑆1⑆10000 20⑆    ⑆⑆296587 7⑈

32-2/1110

**DEPOSIT TICKET**
USE OTHER SIDE FOR ADDITIONAL LISTING

BE SURE EACH ITEM IS PROPERLY ENDORSED

| C A S H | CURRENCY | | |
|---|---|---|---|
| | COIN | | |
| CHECKS (LIST SINGLY) Brown | | 2,396 | 02 |
| TOTAL from reverse side | | | |
| **TOTAL** | | | |
| LESS CASH RECEIVED | | 396 | 02 |
| **NET DEPOSIT** | | 2,000 | 00 |

FOR CLASSROOM USE ONLY

---

# III-24

**HUANG AND HUANG**
7946 WALNUT HILL
DALLAS, TX 75230

DATE ___May 17___ 19 __

SIGN HERE FOR LESS CASH RECEIVED

**Midtown Bank**
Dallas, Texas

⑈ ⑆1⑆10000 20⑆    ⑆⑆493682 5⑈

32-2/1110

**DEPOSIT TICKET**
USE OTHER SIDE FOR ADDITIONAL LISTING

BE SURE EACH ITEM IS PROPERLY ENDORSED

| C A S H | CURRENCY | | |
|---|---|---|---|
| | COIN | 986 | 00 |
| | | 108 | 16 |
| CHECKS (LIST SINGLY) 218 | | 5,426 | 79 |
| 153 | | 33 | 18 |
| 644 | | 214 | 69 |
| TOTAL from reverse side | | | |
| **TOTAL** | | | |
| LESS CASH RECEIVED | | | |
| **NET DEPOSIT** | | 6,768 | 72 |

FOR CLASSROOM USE ONLY

Please List Each Check Separately

| CHECKS | DOLLARS | CENTS |
|--------|---------|-------|
| 1 | | |
| 2 | | |
| 3 | | |
| 4 | | |
| 5 | | |
| 6 | | |
| 7 | | |
| 8 | | |
| 9 | | |
| 10 | | |
| 11 | | |
| 12 | | |
| 13 | | |
| 14 | | |
| 15 | | |
| 16 | | |
| **TOTAL THIS SIDE** ENTER THIS TOTAL ON REVERSE SIDE | | |

Please List Each Check Separately

| CHECKS | DOLLARS | CENTS |
|--------|---------|-------|
| 1 | | |
| 2 | | |
| 3 | | |
| 4 | | |
| 5 | | |
| 6 | | |
| 7 | | |
| 8 | | |
| 9 | | |
| 10 | | |
| 11 | | |
| 12 | | |
| 13 | | |
| 14 | | |
| 15 | | |
| 16 | | |
| **TOTAL THIS SIDE** ENTER THIS TOTAL ON REVERSE SIDE | | |

Please List Each Check Separately

| CHECKS | DOLLARS | CENTS |
|--------|---------|-------|
| 1 | | |
| 2 | | |
| 3 | | |
| 4 | | |
| 5 | | |
| 6 | | |
| 7 | | |
| 8 | | |
| 9 | | |
| 10 | | |
| 11 | | |
| 12 | | |
| 13 | | |
| 14 | | |
| 15 | | |
| 16 | | |
| **TOTAL THIS SIDE** ENTER THIS TOTAL ON REVERSE SIDE | | |

Please List Each Check Separately

| CHECKS | DOLLARS | CENTS |
|--------|---------|-------|
| 1 | | |
| 2 | | |
| 3 | | |
| 4 | | |
| 5 | | |
| 6 | | |
| 7 | | |
| 8 | | |
| 9 | | |
| 10 | | |
| 11 | | |
| 12 | | |
| 13 | | |
| 14 | | |
| 15 | | |
| 16 | | |
| **TOTAL THIS SIDE** ENTER THIS TOTAL ON REVERSE SIDE | | |

Please List Each Check Separately

| CHECKS | DOLLARS | CENTS |
|--------|---------|-------|
| 1 | | |
| 2 | | |
| 3 | | |
| 4 | | |
| 5 | | |
| 6 | | |
| 7 | | |
| 8 | | |
| 9 | | |
| 10 | | |
| 11 | | |
| 12 | | |
| 13 | | |
| 14 | | |
| 15 | | |
| 16 | | |
| **TOTAL THIS SIDE** ENTER THIS TOTAL ON REVERSE SIDE | | |

Please List Each Check Separately

| CHECKS | DOLLARS | CENTS |
|--------|---------|-------|
| 1 | | |
| 2 | | |
| 3 | | |
| 4 | | |
| 5 | | |
| 6 | | |
| 7 | | |
| 8 | | |
| 9 | | |
| 10 | | |
| 11 | | |
| 12 | | |
| 13 | | |
| 14 | | |
| 15 | | |
| 16 | | |
| **TOTAL THIS SIDE** ENTER THIS TOTAL ON REVERSE SIDE | | |

**SHELLY C. WIEMER**
20 CREEKDALE
RICHARDSON, TX 75080

32-2/1110

DEPOSIT TICKET
USE OTHER SIDE FOR ADDITIONAL LISTING

BE SURE EACH ITEM IS PROPERLY ENDORSED

| | CURRENCY | | |
|---|---|---|---|
| C A S H | COIN | | |
| CHECKS (LIST SINGLY) | | | |
| Plano | | 1,650 | — |
| Tulsa | | 350 | — |
| TOTAL from reverse side | | | |
| **TOTAL** | | 2,000 | — |
| LESS CASH RECEIVED | | | |
| **NET DEPOSIT** | | 2,000 | — |

FOR CLASSROOM USE ONLY

DATE  May 17  19 —

SIGN HERE FOR LESS CASH RECEIVED

**Midtown Bank** Dallas, Texas

⑆110000 20⑆ ⑆4 2 6846⑈

---

**MONIQUE OR EDWARD V. GOODMAN**
6893 CONCORD DR.
DALLAS, TX 75150

32-2/1110

DEPOSIT TICKET
USE OTHER SIDE FOR ADDITIONAL LISTING

BE SURE EACH ITEM IS PROPERLY ENDORSED

| | CURRENCY | | |
|---|---|---|---|
| C A S H | COIN | | |
| CHECKS (LIST SINGLY) | | | |
| Moore | | 150 | 00 |
| TOTAL from reverse side | | | |
| **TOTAL** | | 150 | 00 |
| LESS CASH RECEIVED | | | |
| **NET DEPOSIT** | | 150 | 00 |

FOR CLASSROOM USE ONLY

DATE  May 17  19 —

SIGN HERE FOR LESS CASH RECEIVED

**Midtown Bank** Dallas, Texas

⑆110000 20⑆ ⑆443 278 6⑈

---

**BENJAMIN M. AND DOROTHY S. RICHARDSON**
9968 NANCY LANE
DALLAS, TX 75134

32-2/1110

DEPOSIT TICKET
USE OTHER SIDE FOR ADDITIONAL LISTING

BE SURE EACH ITEM IS PROPERLY ENDORSED

| | CURRENCY | | |
|---|---|---|---|
| C A S H | COIN | | |
| CHECKS (LIST SINGLY) | | | |
| 06943 | | 76 | 98 |
| TOTAL from reverse side | | | |
| **TOTAL** | | 76 | 98 |
| LESS CASH RECEIVED | | 26 | 98 |
| **NET DEPOSIT** | | 50 | 00 |

FOR CLASSROOM USE ONLY

DATE  May 17  19 —

Benjamin M. Richardson

SIGN HERE FOR LESS CASH RECEIVED

**Midtown Bank** Dallas, Texas

⑆110000 20⑆ ⑆36 6 5974⑈

---

**JULIE A. PANNELL, A MINOR**
8290 BRASWELL ST.
DALLAS, TX 75231

32-2/1110

DEPOSIT TICKET
USE OTHER SIDE FOR ADDITIONAL LISTING

BE SURE EACH ITEM IS PROPERLY ENDORSED

| | CURRENCY | | |
|---|---|---|---|
| C A S H | CURRENCY | 25 | 00 |
| | COIN | 5 | 45 |
| CHECKS (LIST SINGLY) | | | |
| TOTAL from reverse side | | | |
| **TOTAL** | | 30 | 45 |
| LESS CASH RECEIVED | | | |
| **NET DEPOSIT** | | 30 | 45 |

FOR CLASSROOM USE ONLY

DATE  May 17  19 —

SIGN HERE FOR LESS CASH RECEIVED

**Midtown Bank** Dallas, Texas

⑆110000 20⑆ ⑆69 4368 2⑈

---

**DEWEY E. SCOTT**
2168 NORTHWEST DR.
DALLAS, TX 75150

32-2/1110

DEPOSIT TICKET
USE OTHER SIDE FOR ADDITIONAL LISTING

BE SURE EACH ITEM IS PROPERLY ENDORSED

| | CURRENCY | | |
|---|---|---|---|
| C A S H | COIN | | |
| CHECKS (LIST SINGLY) | | | |
| Dallas | | 1,497 | 50 |
| Ft. Worth | | 50 | 00 |
| TOTAL from reverse side | | | |
| **TOTAL** | | 1,547 | 50 |
| LESS CASH RECEIVED | | 47 | 50 |
| **NET DEPOSIT** | | 1,500 | 00 |

FOR CLASSROOM USE ONLY

DATE  May 17  19 —

Dewey E. Scott

SIGN HERE FOR LESS CASH RECEIVED

**Midtown Bank** Dallas, Texas

⑆110000 20⑆ ⑆56 6386 2⑈

---

**SECURE STORAGE**
1843 W. NW HIGHWAY
DALLAS, TX 75226

32-2/1110

DEPOSIT TICKET
USE OTHER SIDE FOR ADDITIONAL LISTING

BE SURE EACH ITEM IS PROPERLY ENDORSED

| | CURRENCY | | |
|---|---|---|---|
| C A S H | CURRENCY | 1,500 | 00 |
| | COIN | 253 | 00 |
| CHECKS (LIST SINGLY) | | | |
| Adams | | 12,106 | 95 |
| Johnson | | 5,286 | 03 |
| Smith | | 92 | 00 |
| TOTAL from reverse side | | | |
| **TOTAL** | | 19,237 | 98 |
| LESS CASH RECEIVED | | | |
| **NET DEPOSIT** | | 19,237 | 98 |

FOR CLASSROOM USE ONLY

DATE  May 17  19 —

SIGN HERE FOR LESS CASH RECEIVED

**Midtown Bank** Dallas, Texas

⑆110000 20⑆ ⑆33846 68⑈

| CHECKS | DOLLARS | CENTS |
|---|---|---|
| 1 | | |
| 2 | | |
| 3 | | |
| 4 | | |
| 5 | | |
| 6 | | |
| 7 | | |
| 8 | | |
| 9 | | |
| 10 | | |
| 11 | | |
| 12 | | |
| 13 | | |
| 14 | | |
| 15 | | |
| 16 | | |
| **TOTAL THIS SIDE** ENTER THIS TOTAL ON REVERSE SIDE | | |

| CHECKS | DOLLARS | CENTS |
|---|---|---|
| 1 | | |
| 2 | | |
| 3 | | |
| 4 | | |
| 5 | | |
| 6 | | |
| 7 | | |
| 8 | | |
| 9 | | |
| 10 | | |
| 11 | | |
| 12 | | |
| 13 | | |
| 14 | | |
| 15 | | |
| 16 | | |
| **TOTAL THIS SIDE** ENTER THIS TOTAL ON REVERSE SIDE | | |

| CHECKS | DOLLARS | CENTS |
|---|---|---|
| 1 | | |
| 2 | | |
| 3 | | |
| 4 | | |
| 5 | | |
| 6 | | |
| 7 | | |
| 8 | | |
| 9 | | |
| 10 | | |
| 11 | | |
| 12 | | |
| 13 | | |
| 14 | | |
| 15 | | |
| 16 | | |
| **TOTAL THIS SIDE** ENTER THIS TOTAL ON REVERSE SIDE | | |

| CHECKS | DOLLARS | CENTS |
|---|---|---|
| 1 | | |
| 2 | | |
| 3 | | |
| 4 | | |
| 5 | | |
| 6 | | |
| 7 | | |
| 8 | | |
| 9 | | |
| 10 | | |
| 11 | | |
| 12 | | |
| 13 | | |
| 14 | | |
| 15 | | |
| 16 | | |
| **TOTAL THIS SIDE** ENTER THIS TOTAL ON REVERSE SIDE | | |

| CHECKS | DOLLARS | CENTS |
|---|---|---|
| 1 | | |
| 2 | | |
| 3 | | |
| 4 | | |
| 5 | | |
| 6 | | |
| 7 | | |
| 8 | | |
| 9 | | |
| 10 | | |
| 11 | | |
| 12 | | |
| 13 | | |
| 14 | | |
| 15 | | |
| 16 | | |
| **TOTAL THIS SIDE** ENTER THIS TOTAL ON REVERSE SIDE | | |

| CHECKS | DOLLARS | CENTS |
|---|---|---|
| 1 | | |
| 2 | | |
| 3 | | |
| 4 | | |
| 5 | | |
| 6 | | |
| 7 | | |
| 8 | | |
| 9 | | |
| 10 | | |
| 11 | | |
| 12 | | |
| 13 | | |
| 14 | | |
| 15 | | |
| 16 | | |
| **TOTAL THIS SIDE** ENTER THIS TOTAL ON REVERSE SIDE | | |

## A

### SIMULATED CASH RECEIVED

**Currency:**

| | Count | Amount |
|---|---|---|
| Hundreds | 2 | $ 200.00 |
| Fifties | 1 | $ 50.00 |
| Twenties | 16 | $ 320.00 |
| Tens | 39 | $ 390.00 |
| Fives | 28 | $ 140.00 |
| Ones | 44 | $ 44.00 |
| **Total Currency** | | $ 1,144.00 |

**Coins:**

| | Count | Amount |
|---|---|---|
| Dollars | | $ |
| Halves | | $ |
| Quarters | 15 | $ 3.75 |
| Dimes | 28 | $ 2.80 |
| Nickels | 21 | $ 1.05 |
| Pennies | 43 | $ .43 |
| **Total Coins** | | $ 8.03 |
| **TOTAL CASH RECEIVED** | | $ 1,152.03 |

(To Teller Drawer)

## B

### SIMULATED CASH RECEIVED

**Currency:**

| | Count | Amount |
|---|---|---|
| Hundreds | | $ |
| Fifties | | $ |
| Twenties | 2 | $ 40.00 |
| Tens | 3 | $ 30.00 |
| Fives | 3 | $ 15.00 |
| Ones | 2 | $ 2.00 |
| **Total Currency** | | $ 87.00 |

**Coins:**

| | Count | Amount |
|---|---|---|
| Dollars | | $ |
| Halves | 3 | $ 1.50 |
| Quarters | 7 | $ 1.75 |
| Dimes | 15 | $ 1.50 |
| Nickels | 14 | $ .70 |
| Pennies | | $ |
| **Total Coins** | | $ 5.45 |
| **TOTAL CASH RECEIVED** | | $ 92.45 |

(To Teller Drawer)

## C

### SIMULATED CASH FOR DISBURSEMENT

**Currency:**

| | Count | Amount |
|---|---|---|
| Hundreds | | $ |
| Fifties | | $ |
| Twenties | 8 | $ |
| Tens | 6 | $ |
| Fives | 4 | $ |
| Ones | 10 | $ |
| **Total Currency** | | $ |

**Coins:**

| | Count | Amount |
|---|---|---|
| Dollars | | $ |
| Halves | | $ |
| Quarters | | $ |
| Dimes | | $ |
| Nickels | | $ |
| Pennies | | $ |
| **Total Coins** | | $ |
| **TOTAL CASH DISBURSED** | | $ |

(To Customer)

## D

### SIMULATED CASH RECEIVED

**Currency:**

| | Count | Amount |
|---|---|---|
| Hundreds | 2 | $ 200.00 |
| Fifties | 3 | $ 150.00 |
| Twenties | 15 | $ 300.00 |
| Tens | 1 strap | $ 500.00 |
| Fives | 2 straps | $ 500.00 |
| Ones | 5 straps | $ 250.00 |
| **Total Currency** | | $ 1,900.00 |

**Coins:**

| | Count | Amount |
|---|---|---|
| Dollars | 6 | $ 6.00 |
| Halves | 1 roll | $ 10.00 |
| Quarters | 3 rolls | $ 30.00 |
| Dimes | 5 rolls | $ 25.00 |
| Nickels | 4 rolls | $ 8.00 |
| Pennies | 9 rolls | $ 4.50 |
| **Total Coins** | | $ 83.50 |
| **TOTAL CASH RECEIVED** | | $ 1,983.50 |

(To Teller Drawer)

## E

### SIMULATED CASH FOR DISBURSEMENT

**Currency:**

| | Count | Amount |
|---|---|---|
| Hundreds | 2 | $ |
| Fifties | | $ |
| Twenties | 5 | $ |
| Tens | 10 | $ |
| Fives | 5 | $ |
| Ones | 10 | $ |
| **Total Currency** | | $ |

**Coins:**

| | Count | Amount |
|---|---|---|
| Dollars | | $ |
| Halves | 1 | $ |
| Quarters | 1 | $ |
| Dimes | 1 | $ |
| Nickels | | $ |
| Pennies | 4 | $ |
| **Total Coins** | | $ |
| **TOTAL CASH DISBURSED** | | $ |

(To Customer)

## F

### SIMULATED CASH RECEIVED

**Currency:**

| | Count | Amount |
|---|---|---|
| Hundreds | | $ |
| Fifties | 1 | $ 50.00 |
| Twenties | 1 | $ 20.00 |
| Tens | 1 | $ 10.00 |
| Fives | 5 | $ 25.00 |
| Ones | 16 | $ 16.00 |
| **Total Currency** | | $ 121.00 |

**Coins:**

| | Count | Amount |
|---|---|---|
| Dollars | | $ |
| Halves | 6 | $ 3.00 |
| Quarters | 35 | $ 8.75 |
| Dimes | 46 | $ 4.60 |
| Nickels | 28 | $ 1.40 |
| Pennies | 1 roll | $ .50 |
| **Total Coins** | | $ 18.25 |
| **TOTAL CASH RECEIVED** | | $ 139.25 |

(To Teller Drawer)

## SIMULATED CASH FOR DISBURSEMENT

**Currency:**

| | | |
|---|---|---|
| 2 | Hundreds | $ |
| 2 | Fifties | $ |
| 18 | Twenties | $ |
| 6 | Tens | $ |
| 14 | Fives | $ |
| 2 straps | Ones | $ |

**Total Currency** $ _____

**Coins:**

| | | |
|---|---|---|
| 1 roll | Dollars | $ |
| | Halves | $ |
| 2 rolls | Quarters | $ |
| 3 rolls | Dimes | $ |
| 2 rolls | Nickels | $ |
| 6 rolls | Pennies | $ |

**Total Coins** $ _____

**TOTAL CASH DISBURSED** $ _____

(To Customer)

## SIMULATED CASH RECEIVED

**Currency:**

| | | | |
|---|---|---|---|
| 1 | Hundreds | $ | 100.00 |
| 1 | Fifties | $ | 50.00 |
| 3 | Twenties | $ | 60.00 |
| 5 | Tens | $ | 50.00 |
| 10 | Fives | $ | 50.00 |
| 33 | Ones | $ | 33.00 |

**Total Currency** $ 343.00

**Coins:**

| | | | |
|---|---|---|---|
| | Dollars | $ | |
| 4 rolls+4 | Halves | $ | 42.00 |
| 3 rolls+9 | Quarters | $ | 32.25 |
| 4 rolls+27 | Dimes | $ | 22.70 |
| 4 rolls+23 | Nickels | $ | 9.15 |
| 3 | Pennies | $ | .03 |

**Total Coins** $ 106.13

**TOTAL CASH RECEIVED** $ 449.13

(To Teller Drawer)

## SIMULATED CASH RECEIVED

**Currency:**

| | | | |
|---|---|---|---|
| 1 | Hundreds | $ | 100.00 |
| | Fifties | $ | |
| 14 | Twenties | $ | 280.00 |
| 26 | Tens | $ | 280.00 |
| 48 | Fives | $ | 240.00 |
| 11 straps+38 | Ones | $ | 588.00 |

**Total Currency** $ 1,488.00

**Coins:**

| | | | |
|---|---|---|---|
| 4 | Dollars | $ | |
| | Halves | $ | 2.00 |
| 1 roll+18 | Quarters | $ | 14.50 |
| 3 rolls+33 | Dimes | $ | 18.30 |
| 1 roll+34 | Nickels | $ | 3.70 |
| 4 rolls+19 | Pennies | $ | 2.19 |

**Total Coins** $ 40.69

**TOTAL CASH RECEIVED** $ 1,528.69

(To Teller Drawer)

## SIMULATED CASH FOR DISBURSEMENT

**Currency:**

| | | |
|---|---|---|
| 1 | Hundreds | $ |
| 2 | Fifties | $ |
| 16 | Twenties | $ |
| 28 | Tens | $ |
| 56 | Fives | $ |
| 32 | Ones | $ |

**Total Currency** $ _____

**Coins:**

| | | |
|---|---|---|
| 2 | Dollars | $ |
| 12 | Halves | $ |
| 6 rolls | Quarters | $ |
| 6 rolls | Dimes | $ |
| 6 rolls | Nickels | $ |
| 6 rolls | Pennies | $ |

**Total Coins** $ _____

**TOTAL CASH DISBURSED** $ _____

(To Customer)

# TALLY SHEET

**DATE** _____

**(IV)**

| (1) $ Denominations | (2) Total Cash Brought Forward | (3) Transactions + or – | | | | | | | | | | | | | | | | | | | | (4) = Total $ |
|---|---|---|---|---|---|---|---|---|---|---|---|---|---|---|---|---|---|---|---|---|---|---|
| **BILLS:** Hundreds $100 | | | | | | | | | | | | | | | | | | | | | | |
| Fifties $50 | | | | | | | | | | | | | | | | | | | | | | |
| Twenties $20 | | | | | | | | | | | | | | | | | | | | | | |
| Tens $10 | | | | | | | | | | | | | | | | | | | | | | |
| Fives $5 | | | | | | | | | | | | | | | | | | | | | | |
| Ones $1 | | | | | | | | | | | | | | | | | | | | | | |
| **COINS:** Dollars $1 | | | | | | | | | | | | | | | | | | | | | | |
| Halves .50 | | | | | | | | | | | | | | | | | | | | | | |
| Quarters .25 | | | | | | | | | | | | | | | | | | | | | | |
| Dimes .10 | | | | | | | | | | | | | | | | | | | | | | |
| Nickels .05 | | | | | | | | | | | | | | | | | | | | | | |
| Pennies .01 | | | | | | | | | | | | | | | | | | | | | | |

(5) Total Cash

(6) Minus (–) Amount Transferred to Vault Account at Closing

(7) Cash Brought Forward

# TALLY SHEET

DATE _____

(v)

| (1) $ Denominations | (2) Total Cash Brought Forward | (3) Transactions + or – | | | | | | | | | | | | | | | | (4) = Total $ |
|---|---|---|---|---|---|---|---|---|---|---|---|---|---|---|---|---|---|---|
| **BILLS:** Hundreds $100 | 2,000 | | | | | | | | | | | | | | | | | |
| Fifties $50 | 200 | | | | | | | | | | | | | | | | | |
| Twenties $20 | 1,700 | | | | | | | | | | | | | | | | | |
| Tens $10 | 500 | | | | | | | | | | | | | | | | | |
| Fives $5 | 250 | | | | | | | | | | | | | | | | | |
| Ones $1 | 225 | | | | | | | | | | | | | | | | | |
| **COINS:** Dollars $1 | 5 | | | | | | | | | | | | | | | | | |
| Halves .50 | 16 | | | | | | | | | | | | | | | | | |
| Quarters .25 | 50 | | | | | | | | | | | | | | | | | |
| Dimes .10 | 35 | | | | | | | | | | | | | | | | | |
| Nickels .05 | 15 | | | | | | | | | | | | | | | | | |
| Pennies .01 | 4 | | | | | | | | | | | | | | | | | |
| | 5,000 | | | | | | | | | | | | | | | | | |

(5) Total Cash

(6) Minus (–) Amount Transferred to Vault Account at Closing

(7) Cash Brought Forward

## V-1 — Check 1219

JRL Electronics
P.O. Box 6783D
Addison, Texas 75225

1219
192-41/1119

May 15 19 - -

PAY TO THE ORDER OF  Robert J. Bakula      $1,946.28

One Thousand Nine Hundred Forty-six and 28/100 DOLLARS

**Addison Bank**
Addison, Texas

MEMO  Pay Period 1-15 to 1-30-19-    Sally Anders  Treasurer

⑈⑆1190048⑆⑈1219⑈57296617⑈

## V-2 — Check 1523

EARL L. AND AMY S. EDDINGS
7427 ANTHONY DRIVE
DALLAS, TX 75150

1523
32-2/1110

May 17 19 - -

PAY TO THE ORDER OF  Cash      $100.00

One hundred and no/100 ——— DOLLARS

**Midtown Bank**
Dallas, Texas

FOR

Amy S. Eddings
Earl L. Eddings

⑈110000020⑆1523⑈69443 28⑈

## V-3 — Deposit Ticket

MAURICIO I. ALVAREZ
2514 HANOVER ST.
DALLAS, TX 75240

32-2/1110

DEPOSIT TICKET

USE OTHER SIDE FOR ADDITIONAL LISTING

BE SURE EACH ITEM IS PROPERLY ENDORSED

DATE  May 17    19 - -

| | CURRENCY | | |
|---|---|---|---|
| C A S H | COIN | | |
| CHECKS (LIST SINGLY) | | 759 | 23 |
| | | 1,216 | 54 |
| TOTAL from reverse side | | | |
| TOTAL | | | |
| LESS CASH RECEIVED | | | |
| NET DEPOSIT | | 1,975 | 77 |

FOR CLASSROOM USE ONLY

**Midtown Bank**
Dallas, Texas

⑈110000020⑆ ⑈396503⑈

## V-1 — Deposit Ticket

ROBERT J. BAKULA
3719 MAPLEHILL DR.
DALLAS, TX 75150

32-2/1110

DEPOSIT TICKET

USE OTHER SIDE FOR ADDITIONAL LISTING

BE SURE EACH ITEM IS PROPERLY ENDORSED

DATE  MAY 17   19 - -

| | CURRENCY | | |
|---|---|---|---|
| C A S H | COIN | | |
| CHECKS (LIST SINGLY) | 1219 | 1,946 | 28 |
| | 926 | 100 | 00 |
| | 1649 | 18 | 46 |
| TOTAL from reverse side | | | |
| TOTAL | | | |
| LESS CASH RECEIVED | | | |
| NET DEPOSIT | | 2,064 | 74 |

FOR CLASSROOM USE ONLY

**Midtown Bank**
Dallas, Texas

⑈110000020⑆ ⑈693483 ⑈

## V-1 — Check 1649

MELE LUHNOW
5939 BERWYN
DALLAS, TEXAS 75214

1649
32-866/1110

May 8 19 - -

PAY TO THE ORDER OF  Robert Bakula      $18.46

Eighteen and 46/100 ——— DOLLARS

**Dallas County Credit Union**  Dallas, Texas

FOR

Mele Luhnow

⑈11008668⑆1649⑈7735190 76⑈

## V-1 — Check 0926

GLORIA HULSE
5629 SEAGROVE
DALLAS, TEXAS 75243

0926
32-29/1110

May 15 19 - -

PAY TO THE ORDER OF  Bob Bakula      $100.00

One hundred and no/100 ——— DOLLARS

**CNB COMMUNITY NATIONAL BANK**
Dallas, Texas

FOR

G. Hulse

⑈110000295⑆0926⑈4839203 5⑈

Please List Each Check Separately

| | CHECKS | DOLLARS | CENTS |
|---|---|---|---|
| 1 | | | |
| 2 | | | |
| 3 | | | |
| 4 | | | |
| 5 | | | |
| 6 | | | |
| 7 | | | |
| 8 | | | |
| 9 | | | |
| 10 | | | |
| 11 | | | |
| 12 | | | |
| 13 | | | |
| 14 | | | |
| 15 | | | |
| 16 | | | |
| **TOTAL THIS SIDE** ENTER THIS TOTAL ON REVERSE SIDE | | | |

**ENDORSE HERE**

*Robert Bakula*

**DO NOT WRITE, STAMP OR SIGN BELOW THIS LINE**
RESERVED FOR FINANCIAL INSTITUTION USE*

*FEDERAL RESERVE BOARD OF GOVERNORS REG. CC

**ENDORSE HERE**

*Bob Bakula*

**DO NOT WRITE, STAMP OR SIGN BELOW THIS LINE**
RESERVED FOR FINANCIAL INSTITUTION USE*

*FEDERAL RESERVE BOARD OF GOVERNORS REG. CC

**ENDORSE HERE**

*Robert T. Bakula*

**DO NOT WRITE, STAMP OR SIGN BELOW THIS LINE**
RESERVED FOR FINANCIAL INSTITUTION USE*

*FEDERAL RESERVE BOARD OF GOVERNORS REG. CC

**ENDORSE HERE**

**DO NOT WRITE, STAMP OR SIGN BELOW THIS LINE**
RESERVED FOR FINANCIAL INSTITUTION USE*

*FEDERAL RESERVE BOARD OF GOVERNORS REG. CC

Please List Each Check Separately

| | CHECKS | DOLLARS | CENTS |
|---|---|---|---|
| 1 | | | |
| 2 | | | |
| 3 | | | |
| 4 | | | |
| 5 | | | |
| 6 | | | |
| 7 | | | |
| 8 | | | |
| 9 | | | |
| 10 | | | |
| 11 | | | |
| 12 | | | |
| 13 | | | |
| 14 | | | |
| 15 | | | |
| 16 | | | |
| **TOTAL THIS SIDE** ENTER THIS TOTAL ON REVERSE SIDE | | | |

## SIMULATED CASH FOR DISBURSEMENT (V-7)

| Currency: | | |
|---|---|---|
| Hundreds | $ | |
| Fifties | $ | |
| Twenties | $ | |
| Tens | $ | |
| Fives | $ | |
| Ones | $ | |
| Total Currency | $ | |
| Coins: | | |
| Dollars | $ | |
| Halves | $ | |
| Quarters | $ | |
| Dimes | $ | |
| Nickels | $ | |
| Pennies | $ | |
| Total Coins | | |
| TOTAL CASH DISBURSED | $ | |

(To Customer)

## SIMULATED CASH RECEIVED (V-8)

| Currency: | | |
|---|---|---|
| Hundreds | 1 | $ 100.00 |
| Fifties | | $ |
| Twenties | 26 | $ 520.00 |
| Tens | 34 | $ 340.00 |
| Fives | 52 | $ 260.00 |
| Ones | 113 | $ 113.00 |
| Total Currency | | $ 1,333.00 |
| Coins: | | |
| Dollars | | $ |
| Halves | | $ |
| Quarters | 6 rolls | $ 60.00 |
| Dimes | 4 rolls | $ 20.00 |
| Nickels | 3 rolls | $ 6.00 |
| Pennies | 1 roll | $ 3.50 |
| Total Coins | | $ 89.50 |
| TOTAL CASH RECEIVED | | $ 1,422.50 |

(To Teller Drawer)

## SIMULATED CASH FOR DISBURSEMENT (V-5)

| Currency: | | |
|---|---|---|
| Hundreds | $ | |
| Fifties | $ | |
| Twenties | $ | |
| Tens | $ | |
| Fives | $ | |
| Ones | $ | |
| Total Currency | $ | |
| Coins: | | |
| Dollars | $ | |
| Halves | $ | |
| Quarters | $ | |
| Dimes | $ | |
| Nickels | $ | |
| Pennies | $ | |
| Total Coins | | |
| TOTAL CASH DISBURSED | $ | |

(To Customer)

## SIMULATED CASH RECEIVED (V-5)

| Currency: | | |
|---|---|---|
| Hundreds | 1 | $ 100.00 |
| Fifties | | $ |
| Twenties | | $ |
| Tens | | $ |
| Fives | | $ |
| Ones | | $ |
| Total Currency | | $ 100.00 |
| Coins: | | |
| Dollars | | $ |
| Halves | | $ |
| Quarters | | $ |
| Dimes | | $ |
| Nickels | | $ |
| Pennies | | $ |
| Total Coins | | |
| TOTAL CASH RECEIVED | | $ 100.00 |

(To Teller Drawer)

## SIMULATED CASH FOR DISBURSEMENT (V-2)

| Currency: | | |
|---|---|---|
| Hundreds | $ | |
| Fifties | $ | |
| Twenties | $ | |
| Tens | $ | |
| Fives | $ | |
| Ones | $ | |
| Total Currency | $ | |
| Coins: | | |
| Dollars | $ | |
| Halves | $ | |
| Quarters | $ | |
| Dimes | $ | |
| Nickels | $ | |
| Pennies | $ | |
| Total Coins | | |
| TOTAL CASH DISBURSED | $ | |

(To Customer)

## SIMULATED CASH RECEIVED (V-4)

| Currency: | | |
|---|---|---|
| Hundreds | | $ |
| Fifties | | $ |
| Twenties | 3 | $ 60.00 |
| Tens | 2 | $ 20.00 |
| Fives | 4 | $ 20.00 |
| Ones | | $ |
| Total Currency | | $ 100.00 |
| Coins: | | |
| Dollars | | $ |
| Halves | | $ |
| Quarters | | $ |
| Dimes | | $ |
| Nickels | | $ |
| Pennies | | $ |
| Total Coins | | |
| TOTAL CASH RECEIVED | | $ 100.00 |

(To Teller Drawer)

## REQUEST FOR CUSTOMER INFORMATION  (V-4)

Name _____

Acct. No. _____

Acct. Type _____

Last Deposit _____

Comments _____

---

## ALUMAX MANAGEMENT SYSTEMS  (0658) (V-3)
2611 STEMMONS
DALLAS, TX 75258

32-1076/1110

May 12  19 - -

PAY TO THE ORDER OF _Maurice Alvarez_  $1216 54/

_One thousand two hundred sixteen and 54/100_ DOLLARS

**S**ECURITY **FIRST BANK**
DALLAS, TEXAS

FOR CLASSROOM USE ONLY

FOR _____

⑈1110107068⑈:0658⑈674829⑈6⑈

---

## METCALF OIL AND GAS  (2839) (V-3)
5783 CLEARFIELD DR.
DALLAS, TX 75043

32-934/1110

May 13  19 - -

PAY TO THE ORDER OF _Maurice Cisneros_  $759.23

_Seven hundred fifty-nine and 23/100_ DOLLARS

**Dallas METROPLEX Bank**
Dallas, Texas

FOR CLASSROOM USE ONLY

FOR _____

D. L. Metcalf

⑈11100934⑈5:2839⑈6839700 24⑈

---

## DEPOSIT TICKET  (V-6)

32-2/1110

| C A S H | CURRENCY | | |
|---|---|---|---|
| | COIN | | |
| CHECKS (LIST SINGLY) | | | |
| | | 1512 | 394 73 |
| | | 1346 | 441 27 |
| TOTAL from reverse side | | | 390 99 |
| **TOTAL** | | | 1,226 99 |
| LESS CASH RECEIVED | | | |
| **NET DEPOSIT** | | | 1,226 99 |

USE OTHER SIDE FOR ADDITIONAL LISTING

**DEPOSIT TICKET**

BE SURE EACH ITEM IS PROPERLY ENDORSED

**CASEY'S CREATIONS**
18691 INDUSTRIAL, SUITE 2A
DALLAS, TX 75205

DATE  May 17  19 - -

SIGN HERE FOR LESS CASH RECEIVED

FOR CLASSROOM USE ONLY

**Midtown Bank**
Dallas, Texas

⑈111000020⑈:  "⑈4965878⑈"

---

## KEITH MYERS INSURANCE  (1634) (V-4)
19543 COTTONWOOD ROAD
RICHARDSON, TX 75080

362-6/1119

May 13  19 - -

PAY TO THE ORDER OF _Alberto J. Suarez_  $500.00

_Five hundred and no/100_ DOLLARS

**1** **BANK AND TRUST**
RICHARDSON ● TEXAS

FOR CLASSROOM USE ONLY

FOR _Claim 346784_

Keith Myers

⑈111900069⑈:1634⑈623896⑈"

---

Loren Leyman  (16853) (V-6)
77543 EastView
Dallas, TX 75081

67-20/1119

May 10  19 - -

Pay to the Order of _Casey's creations_  $63.15

_sixty-three and 15/100_ Dollars

**First Bank of Garland**
Garland, Texas

FOR CLASSROOM USE ONLY

Memo _no acct._

Loren Leyman

⑈111900209⑈:6853⑈384756 29⑈"

Please List Each Check Separately

| | CHECKS | DOLLARS | CENTS |
|---|---|---|---|
| 1 | 514 | 87 | 43 |
| 2 | 1417 | 46 | 12 |
| 3 | 815 | 155 | 80 |
| 4 | 16853 | 63 | 15 |
| 5 | 1682 | 38 | 49 |
| 6 | | | |
| 7 | | | |
| 8 | | | |
| 9 | | | |
| 10 | | | |
| 11 | | | |
| 12 | | | |
| 13 | | | |
| 14 | | | |
| 15 | | | |
| 16 | | | |
| TOTAL THIS SIDE ENTER THIS TOTAL ON REVERSE SIDE | | 390 | 99 |

**0815** V-6

CLAUDIA J. HALL
6743 IDAHO
DALLAS, TX 75216

May 12 19 --

32-2/1110

PAY TO THE ORDER OF _Casey's Creations_ $155.80

_One hundred fifty-five and 80/100_ ——— DOLLARS

**Midtown Bank**
Dallas, Texas

FOR _____

⑈1110000 20⑈081 5⑈ 56 2 9645⑈

FOR CLASSROOM USE ONLY

_Claudia J. Hall_

---

**1682** V-6

CHERYL M. OR A. J. ROBERSON
7854 LEGENDERY LANE
DALLAS, TX 75224

May 15 19 --

32-534/1110

PAY TO THE ORDER OF _Casey's Creations_ $38.49

_Thirty-eight and 49/100_ ——— DOLLARS

**DALLAS BANK**
DALLAS, TEXAS

FOR _____

⑈1100 534⑈ 168 2⑈ 6735 2689⑈

FOR CLASSROOM USE ONLY

_A. J. Roberson_

---

**0514** V-6

Russell P. Denman
2843 Moser
Dallas, Texas 75206

May 14 19 --

32-2571/1110

PAY TO THE ORDER OF _Casey's Creations_ $87.43

_Eighty-seven and 43/100_ ——— DOLLARS

**Dallas County Bank**
Dallas, Texas

FOR _Inv 16942_

⑈110 257⑈ 0⑈05 4⑈ 7634 298⑈

FOR CLASSROOM USE ONLY

_Russell P. Denman_

---

**1417** V-6

ARTHUR OR JEANNETTE MAULDIN
8222 SARATOGA CIRCLE
DALLAS, TEXAS 75214

May 16 19 --

32-29/1110

PAY TO THE ORDER OF _Casey's Creations_ $46.12

_Forty-six and 12/100_ ——— DOLLARS

**CNB** COMMUNITY
NATIONAL BANK
Dallas, Texas

FOR _____

⑈1110000 29⑈ 1 4 17⑈ 6643 2789⑈

FOR CLASSROOM USE ONLY

_Jeannette Mauldin_

---

**1512** V-6

DOROTHY OR BRUCE BECERRA
1189 MELROSE DRIVE
DALLAS, TX 75081

May 14 19 --

362-6/1119

PAY TO THE ORDER OF _Casey's Creations_ $394.73

_Three hundred ninety-four and 73/100_ DOLLARS

**1** BANK AND TRUST
RICHARDSON • TEXAS

FOR _Acct. 16-2834_

⑈1190006⑈ 1512⑈ 8407 43⑈

FOR CLASSROOM USE ONLY

_Dorothy Becerra_

---

**1346** V-6

Mr. or Mrs. Brian C. Mitcham
6208 Emery Oak Lane
Dallas, Texas 75249

May 15 19 --

192-41/1119

PAY TO THE ORDER OF _Casey's Creations_ $441.27

_Four hundred forty-one and 27/100_ ——— DOLLARS

**Addison Bank**
Addison, Texas

MEMO _____

⑈1190 0 4⑈8⑈ 1346⑈ 5376903⑈

FOR CLASSROOM USE ONLY

_Brian C. Mitcham_

ENDORSE HERE

*Casey's Creations*
*Acct. 496-587-8*

**DO NOT WRITE, STAMP OR SIGN BELOW THIS LINE**
RESERVED FOR FINANCIAL INSTITUTION USE*

*FEDERAL RESERVE BOARD OF GOVERNORS REG. CC

ENDORSE HERE

*Casey's Creations*
*Acct. 496-587-8*

**DO NOT WRITE, STAMP OR SIGN BELOW THIS LINE**
RESERVED FOR FINANCIAL INSTITUTION USE*

*FEDERAL RESERVE BOARD OF GOVERNORS REG. CC

ENDORSE HERE

*Casey's Creations*
*Acct. 496-587-8*

**DO NOT WRITE, STAMP OR SIGN BELOW THIS LINE**
RESERVED FOR FINANCIAL INSTITUTION USE*

*FEDERAL RESERVE BOARD OF GOVERNORS REG. CC

ENDORSE HERE

*Casey's Creations*
*Acct. 496-587-8*

**DO NOT WRITE, STAMP OR SIGN BELOW THIS LINE**
RESERVED FOR FINANCIAL INSTITUTION USE*

*FEDERAL RESERVE BOARD OF GOVERNORS REG. CC

ENDORSE HERE

*Casey's Creations*
*Acct. 496-587-8*

**DO NOT WRITE, STAMP OR SIGN BELOW THIS LINE**
RESERVED FOR FINANCIAL INSTITUTION USE*

*FEDERAL RESERVE BOARD OF GOVERNORS REG. CC

ENDORSE HERE

*Casey's Creations*
*Acct. 496-587-8*

**DO NOT WRITE, STAMP OR SIGN BELOW THIS LINE**
RESERVED FOR FINANCIAL INSTITUTION USE*

*FEDERAL RESERVE BOARD OF GOVERNORS REG. CC

## Check 1506

TIMOTHY AND ELLEN COX
7808 HANCOCK DRIVE
DALLAS, TX 75204

1506
V-8
32-2/1110

May 14 19 —

PAY TO THE ORDER OF _Louisiana Kitchen_ $ 46.81

_Forty-six and 81/100_ DOLLARS

FOR CLASSROOM USE ONLY

**Midtown Bank**
Dallas, Texas

Ellen Cox
Timothy Cox

FOR ⑆ 1110000 20⑆ 1506 ⑈ 791374 2⑆

---

## Check 0426

WILLIAM OR MARY ALICE MITCHELL
6731 EWING AVENUE
DALLAS, TX 75016

0426
V-8
32-2/1110

May 10 19 —

PAY TO THE ORDER OF _Louisiana Kitchen_ $ 17.93

_Seventeen and 93/100_ DOLLARS

FOR CLASSROOM USE ONLY

**Midtown Bank**
Dallas, Texas

Mary Alice Mitchell

FOR ⑆ 1110000 20⑆ 0426 ⑈ 98 7743⑆

---

## Check 0163

GEORGE T. PASSMORE
56321 LEGRANDE
DALLAS, TEXAS 75244

0163
V-8
32-29/1110

May 11 19 —

PAY TO THE ORDER OF _Louisiana Kitchen_ $ 24.36

_Twenty-four and 36/100_ DOLLARS

FOR CLASSROOM USE ONLY

**CNB** COMMUNITY
NATIONAL BANK
Dallas, Texas

George T. Passmore

FOR ⑆ 1110000 29⑆ 0163 ⑈ 357 8935⑆

---

## Check 1364

JESSICA F. HOUSTON
1503 COLORADO BLVD.
DALLAS, TX 75208

1364
V-7
32-2/1110

May 17 19 —

PAY TO THE ORDER OF _Midtown Bank_ $ 500.00

_Five hundred and 00/100_ DOLLARS

FOR CLASSROOM USE ONLY

**Midtown Bank**
Dallas, Texas

Jessica F. Houston

FOR _Cash_ ⑆ 1110000 20⑆ 1364 ⑈ 296 587⑆

---

## Deposit Ticket

LOUISIANA KITCHEN
605 E. MAIN STREET
DALLAS, TX 75201

V-8

32-2/1110

**DEPOSIT TICKET**

USE OTHER SIDE FOR ADDITIONAL LISTING

BE SURE EACH ITEM IS PROPERLY ENDORSED

DATE _May 17_ 19 — —

SIGN HERE FOR LESS CASH RECEIVED

FOR CLASSROOM USE ONLY

**Midtown Bank**
Dallas, Texas

⑆ 1110000 20⑆ ⑆ 4768427⑆

| | | |
|---|---|---|
| CASH | CURRENCY | 1333 00 |
| | COIN | 89 50 |
| CHECKS (LIST SINGLY) 1134 | | 14 85 |
| 1506 | | 46 81 |
| 529 | | 15 38 |
| TOTAL from reverse side | | 72 85 |
| **TOTAL** | | 1,572 39 |
| LESS CASH RECEIVED | | |
| **NET DEPOSIT** | | 1,572 39 |

---

## Check 0721

RAOUL OR DEBORAH TOOL
734 OGDEN
DALLAS, TX 75211

0721
V-8
32-934/1110

May 12 19 — —

PAY TO THE ORDER OF _Louisiana Kitchen_ $ 30.56

_Thirty and 56/100_ DOLLARS

FOR CLASSROOM USE ONLY

**Dallas METROPLEX Bank**
Dallas, Texas

Raoul Tool

FOR ⑆ 110093 45⑆ 0 721 ⑈ 374 829 18 7⑆

**ENDORSE HERE**

**Please List Each Check Separately**

| | CHECKS | DOLLARS | CENTS |
|---|---|---|---|
| 1 | 721 | 30 | 56 |
| 2 | 426 | 17 | 93 |
| 3 | 163 | 24 | 36 |
| 4 | | | |
| 5 | | | |
| 6 | | | |
| 7 | | | |
| 8 | | | |
| 9 | | | |
| 10 | | | |
| 11 | | | |
| 12 | | | |
| 13 | | | |
| 14 | | | |
| 15 | | | |
| 16 | | | |
| TOTAL THIS SIDE<br>ENTER THIS TOTAL<br>ON REVERSE SIDE | | 72 | 85 |

**ENDORSE HERE**

For deposit

Louisiana Kitchen

**DO NOT WRITE, STAMP OR SIGN BELOW THIS LINE**
RESERVED FOR FINANCIAL INSTITUTION USE*

*FEDERAL RESERVE BOARD OF GOVERNORS REG. CC

**DO NOT WRITE, STAMP OR SIGN BELOW THIS LINE**
RESERVED FOR FINANCIAL INSTITUTION USE*

*FEDERAL RESERVE BOARD OF GOVERNORS REG. CC

**ENDORSE HERE**

For deposit

Louisiana Kitchen

**ENDORSE HERE**

For deposit

Louisiana Kitchen

**ENDORSE HERE**

For deposit

Louisiana Kitchen

**DO NOT WRITE, STAMP OR SIGN BELOW THIS LINE**
RESERVED FOR FINANCIAL INSTITUTION USE*

**DO NOT WRITE, STAMP OR SIGN BELOW THIS LINE**
RESERVED FOR FINANCIAL INSTITUTION USE*

**DO NOT WRITE, STAMP OR SIGN BELOW THIS LINE**
RESERVED FOR FINANCIAL INSTITUTION USE*

*FEDERAL RESERVE BOARD OF GOVERNORS REG. CC

*FEDERAL RESERVE BOARD OF GOVERNORS REG. CC

*FEDERAL RESERVE BOARD OF GOVERNORS REG. CC

# TRANSACTION REQUEST FORM

**Name** Alberto J. Guerrero    **Date**

**Midtown Bank** Dallas, Texas

**Account #** 469-583-3    **Teller**

## DEPOSIT    Acct. Type: Checking ☐ Savings ☒

| | | |
|---|---|---|
| Cash | 100 | 00 |
| Checks | 500 | 00 |
| | | |
| | | |
| | | |
| | | |
| Total Received | 600 | 00 |
| Less Cash Received | | |
| Net Deposit | 600 | 00 |

### WITHDRAWAL

Checking $_____
Savings $_____

### TRANSFER

$_____
From Acct. # _____
To Acct. # _____

**Signature**

---

# TRANSACTION REQUEST FORM

**Name** Phyllis A. Lee    **Date**

**Midtown Bank** Dallas, Texas

**Account #** 841-191-9    **Teller**

## DEPOSIT    Acct. Type: Checking ☐ Savings ☒

| | | |
|---|---|---|
| Cash | 358 | 50 |
| Checks | | |
| | | |
| | | |
| | | |
| | | |
| Total Received | 358 | 50 |
| Less Cash Received | | |
| Net Deposit | 358 | 50 |

### WITHDRAWAL

Checking $_____
Savings $_____

### TRANSFER

$_____
From Acct. # _____
To Acct. # _____

**Signature**

---

# TRANSACTION REQUEST FORM

**Name** Carlos M. Viviano    **Date**

**Midtown Bank** Dallas, Texas

**Account #** 483-461-5    **Teller**

## DEPOSIT    Acct. Type: Checking ☐ Savings ☐

| | | |
|---|---|---|
| Cash | | |
| Checks | | |
| | | |
| | | |
| | | |
| | | |
| Total Received | | |
| Less Cash Received | | |
| Net Deposit | | |

### WITHDRAWAL

Checking $_____
Savings $_____

### TRANSFER

$_____
From Acct. # _____
To Acct. # _____

**Signature**

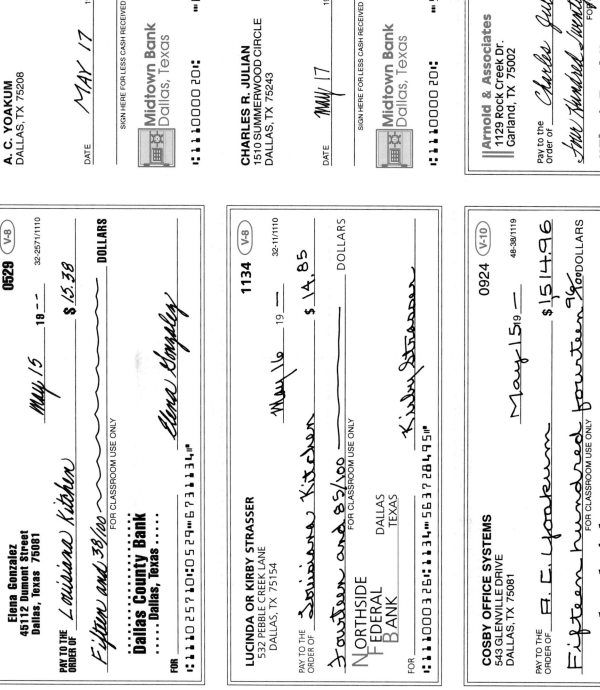

**Deposit Ticket (V-10)**

32-2/1110

DEPOSIT TICKET
USE OTHER SIDE FOR ADDITIONAL LISTING
BE SURE EACH ITEM IS PROPERLY ENDORSED

| C A S H | CURRENCY | | |
|---|---|---|---|
| | COIN | | |
| CHECKS (LIST SINGLY) | | 1,514 | 96 |
| TOTAL from reverse side | | | |
| TOTAL | | 1,514 | 96 |
| LESS CASH RECEIVED | | 85 | — |
| NET DEPOSIT | | 1,429 | 96 |

FOR CLASSROOM USE ONLY

A. C. YOAKUM
DALLAS, TX 75208

DATE MAY 17 19 —

SIGN HERE FOR LESS CASH RECEIVED

Midtown Bank
Dallas, Texas

⑈1110 0000 20⑈ ⑈683945 2⑈

**Deposit Ticket (V-12)**

32-2/1110

DEPOSIT TICKET
USE OTHER SIDE FOR ADDITIONAL LISTING
BE SURE EACH ITEM IS PROPERLY ENDORSED

| C A S H | CURRENCY | | |
|---|---|---|---|
| | COIN | | |
| CHECKS (LIST SINGLY) | cash | 421 | 96 |
| | total | 243 | 57 |
| TOTAL from reverse side | | | |
| TOTAL | | | |
| LESS CASH RECEIVED | | | |
| NET DEPOSIT | | 665 | 53 |

FOR CLASSROOM USE ONLY

CHARLES R. JULIAN
1510 SUMMERWOOD CIRCLE
DALLAS, TX 75243

DATE MAY 17 19 —

SIGN HERE FOR LESS CASH RECEIVED

Midtown Bank
Dallas, Texas

⑈1110 0000 20⑈ ⑈563291 6⑈

**Check 0489 (V-12)**

0489
67-20/1119

Arnold & Associates
1129 Rock Creek Dr.
Garland, TX 75002

May 15 19 —

Pay to the Order of Charles Julian      $ 421.96

Four Hundred twenty-one and 96/100 — Dollars

First Bank of Garland   Garland, Texas

FOR CLASSROOM USE ONLY

Memo _____

Elizabeth Arnold

⑈1119 00 20⑈ 0489⑈ 67 290326⑈

**Check 0529 (V-8)**

0529
32-2571/1110

Elena Gonzalez
45112 Dumont Street
Dallas, Texas 75081

May 15 19 — 

PAY TO THE ORDER OF Louisiana Kitchen      $ 15.38

Fifteen and 38/100 ~~~~~~~~ DOLLARS

Dallas County Bank
Dallas, Texas

FOR CLASSROOM USE ONLY

FOR _____

Elena Gonzalez

⑈1110 2571⑈ 0529⑈ 673134⑈

**Check 1134 (V-8)**

1134
32-11/1110

LUCINDA OR KIRBY STRASSER
532 PEBBLE CREEK LANE
DALLAS, TX 75154

May 16 19 —

PAY TO THE ORDER OF Louisiana Kitchen      $ 14.85

Fourteen and 85/100 ~~~~~~~~ DOLLARS

NORTHSIDE
FEDERAL
BANK     DALLAS    TEXAS

FOR CLASSROOM USE ONLY

FOR _____

Kirby Strasser

⑈1110 0032 6⑈ 1134⑈ 56372849 5⑈

**Check 0924 (V-10)**

0924
48-38/1119

COSBY OFFICE SYSTEMS
543 GLENVILLE DRIVE
DALLAS, TX 75081

May 15 19 —

PAY TO THE ORDER OF A. C. Yoakum      $ 1514.96

Fifteen hundred fourteen and 96/100 DOLLARS

Second Bank of Plano
PLANO, TEXAS

FOR CLASSROOM USE ONLY

FOR _____

O. T. Cosby

⑈1119 0038 5⑈ 0924⑈ 74839 20⑈

Please List Each Check Separately

| CHECKS | DOLLARS | CENTS |
|---|---|---|
| 1 | | |
| 2 | | |
| 3 | | |
| 4 | | |
| 5 | | |
| 6 | | |
| 7 | | |
| 8 | | |
| 9 | | |
| 10 | | |
| 11 | | |
| 12 | | |
| 13 | | |
| 14 | | |
| 15 | | |
| 16 | | |
| TOTAL THIS SIDE ENTER THIS TOTAL ON REVERSE SIDE | | |

Please List Each Check Separately

| CHECKS | DOLLARS | CENTS |
|---|---|---|
| 1 | | |
| 2 | | |
| 3 | | |
| 4 | | |
| 5 | | |
| 6 | | |
| 7 | | |
| 8 | | |
| 9 | | |
| 10 | | |
| 11 | | |
| 12 | | |
| 13 | | |
| 14 | | |
| 15 | | |
| 16 | | |
| TOTAL THIS SIDE ENTER THIS TOTAL ON REVERSE SIDE | | |

# TRANSACTION REQUEST FORM

**Midtown Bank**
Dallas, Texas

**Name** _Holly C. Conley_    **Date** _____

**Account #** _____    **Teller** _____

## DEPOSIT    Acct. Type: Checking ☐    Savings ☐

| | |
|---|---|
| Cash | |
| Checks _____ | |
| _____ | |
| _____ | |
| _____ | |
| _____ | |
| Total Received | |
| Less Cash Received | |
| Net Deposit | |

## WITHDRAWAL

Checking    $_____

Savings    $_____

## TRANSFER

$_____

From Acct. # _456-982-7_

To Acct. # _893-462-1_

**Signature** _____

---

## SIMULATED CASH FOR DISBURSEMENT

Currency:

| | |
|---|---|
| Hundreds | $ |
| Fifties | $ |
| Twenties | $ |
| Tens | $ |
| Fives | $ |
| Ones | $ |

Total Currency $

Coins:

| | |
|---|---|
| Dollars | $ |
| Halves | $ |
| Quarters | $ |
| Dimes | $ |
| Nickels | $ |
| Pennies | $ |

Total Coins $

TOTAL CASH DISBURSED $    (To Customer)

---

## SIMULATED CASH FOR DISBURSEMENT

Currency:

| | |
|---|---|
| Hundreds | $ |
| Fifties | $ |
| Twenties | $ |
| Tens | $ |
| Fives | $ |
| Ones | $ |

Total Currency $

Coins:

| | |
|---|---|
| Dollars | $ |
| Halves | $ |
| Quarters | $ |
| Dimes | $ |
| Nickels | $ |
| Pennies | $ |

Total Coins $

TOTAL CASH DISBURSED $    (To Customer)

---

## SIMULATED CASH RECEIVED

Currency:

| | | |
|---|---|---|
| | Hundreds | $ |
| | Fifties | $ |
| 8 | Twenties | $ 160.00 |
| 5 | Tens | $ 50.00 |
| 16 | Fives | $ 80.00 |
| 35 | Ones | $ 35.00 |

Total Currency $ 325.00

Coins:

| | | |
|---|---|---|
| | Dollars | $ |
| 4 | Halves | $ 2.00 |
| 2 rolls | Quarters | $ 20.00 |
| 1 roll | Dimes | $ 5.00 |
| 2 rolls | Nickels | $ 4.00 |
| 5 rolls | Pennies | $ 2.50 |

Total Coins $ 33.50

TOTAL CASH RECEIVED $ 358.50    (To Teller Drawer)

---

## SIMULATED CASH FOR DISBURSEMENT

Currency:

| | |
|---|---|
| Hundreds | $ |
| Fifties | $ |
| Twenties | $ |
| Tens | $ |
| Fives | $ |
| Ones | $ |

Total Currency $

Coins:

| | |
|---|---|
| Dollars | $ |
| Halves | $ |
| Quarters | $ |
| Dimes | $ |
| Nickels | $ |
| Pennies | $ |

Total Coins $

TOTAL CASH DISBURSED $    (To Customer)

## DEPOSIT TICKET

RONALD D. TERRILL INVESTMENTS
5432 N. HALL ST., SUITE 684
DALLAS, TX 75204

32-2/1110

DATE _May 17_ 19 _—_

USE OTHER SIDE FOR
ADDITIONAL LISTING

BE SURE EACH ITEM IS
PROPERLY ENDORSED

| C | CURRENCY | | |
|---|---|---|---|
| A S H | COIN | | |
| CHECKS (LIST SINGLY) | | 729 | |
| | | 938 | |
| | | 7,483 | 21 |
| | | 3,675 | 14 |
| TOTAL from reverse side | | 5,067 | 13 |
| TOTAL | | 16,225 | 48 |
| LESS CASH RECEIVED | | | |
| NET DEPOSIT | | | |

SIGN HERE FOR LESS CASH RECEIVED

FOR CLASSROOM USE ONLY

**Midtown Bank**
Dallas, Texas

⑆ 1110000 20 ⑆ 104683 2 ⑊

---

3418

SUBURBAN INVESTMENT CLUB
7856 DANNIS ROAD
DALLAS, TX 75229

32-534/1110

_May 15_ 19 _—_

PAY TO THE
ORDER OF _Ronald Terrill Inv._ $ _4,216.35_

_Four thousand two hundred ten and 35/100_ ———— DOLLARS

**DALLAS BANK**
DALLAS, TEXAS

FOR _____

_Ralph Andrus_

⑆ 1100534 ⑆ 5 ⑆ 3418 ⑊ 463 126 78 ⑊

---

2864

Vincent or Susan Eaton
6743 Patria
Dallas, Texas 75149

32-2571/1110

_May 14_ 19 _—_

PAY TO THE
ORDER OF _Ronald D. Terrill Investments_ $ _856.78_

_Eight hundred fifty-six and 78/100_ ———— DOLLARS

**Dallas County Bank**
..... **Dallas, Texas** .....

FOR _____

_Susan Eaton_

⑆ 110257 10 ⑆ 2864 ⑊ 368903 2 ⑊

---

1084

TOWNLEY TREADMILLS
17008 PRESTON RD., SUITE 350D
DALLAS, TEXAS 75240

32-29/1110

_May 16_ 19 _—_

PAY TO THE
ORDER OF _Charles R. Julien_ $ _243.57_

_Two Hundred Forty-three and 57/100_ ———— DOLLARS

FOR CLASSROOM USE ONLY

**CNB** COMMUNITY
NATIONAL BANK
Dallas, Texas

FOR _____

_J. C. Townley_

⑆ 110000 29 ⑆ 1084 ⑊ 452 196 738 ⑊

---

1108

MONIQUE GOODMAN
DALLAS, TEXAS 75150

32-2/1110

_May 17_ 19 _—_

PAY TO THE
ORDER OF _Alexandra Arena_ $ _48.00_

_Forty-eight and no/100_ ———— DOLLARS

FOR CLASSROOM USE ONLY

**Midtown Bank**
Dallas, Texas

FOR _6 hrs. @ $8.00_

_Monique Goodman_

⑆ 110000 20 ⑆ 1108 ⑊ 43 278 1 ⑊

---

## REQUEST FOR CUSTOMER INFORMATION

**Name** _____

**Acct. No.** _____

**Acct. Type** _____

**Last Deposit** _____

**Comments** _____

Charles R. Julian

Please List Each Check Separately

| | CHECKS | DOLLARS | CENTS |
|---|---|---|---|
| 1 | 3418 | 4,210 | 35 |
| 2 | 2864 | 856 | 78 |
| 3 | | | |
| 4 | | | |
| 5 | | | |
| 6 | | | |
| 7 | | | |
| 8 | | | |
| 9 | | | |
| 10 | | | |
| 11 | | | |
| 12 | | | |
| 13 | | | |
| 14 | | | |
| 15 | | | |
| 16 | | | |
| TOTAL THIS SIDE ENTER THIS TOTAL ON REVERSE SIDE | 5,067 | 13 | |

Ronald Terrill Investments
#1046832

Ronald O. Terrill Investments

## REQUEST FOR CUSTOMER INFORMATION  V-17

**Name** _____

**Acct. No.** _____

**Acct. Type** _____

**Last Deposit** _____

**Comments** _____

---

V-17   0880

32-29/1110

ERICA BRUNO
4572 LAFAYETTE DR.
DALLAS, TEXAS 75204

May 15 19 ___

PAY TO THE
ORDER OF _Amanda Humphreys_   $ 95⁰⁰

_Ninety-five and no/100_ ___ DOLLARS

**CNB** COMMUNITY
NATIONAL BANK
Dallas, Texas

FOR CLASSROOM USE ONLY

FOR _____

⑈11000 295⑈0880⑈ 566 37 2930⑈

_Erica Bruno_

---

V-18   DEPOSIT TICKET

32-2/1110

USE OTHER SIDE FOR
ADDITIONAL LISTING

BE SURE EACH ITEM IS
PROPERLY ENDORSED

| C | CURRENCY | 996 | 00 |
| A S H | COIN | 32 | 00 |
| | CHECKS (LIST SINGLY) | 1,086 | 51 |
| | | 17 | 68 |
| | | 67 | 91 |
| | TOTAL from reverse side | 2,452 | 16 |
| | **TOTAL** | 4,652 | 26 |
| | LESS CASH RECEIVED | | |
| | **NET DEPOSIT** | 4,652 | 26 |

C. TYLER MONROE ENTERPRISES
16843 N. INWOOD, SUITE 40
DALLAS, TX 75240

DATE _May 17_ 19 ___

SIGN HERE FOR LESS CASH RECEIVED

**Midtown Bank**
Dallas, Texas

FOR CLASSROOM USE ONLY

⑈11 10000 20⑈   ⑈48698 23⑈

---

V-16   0729

32-2/1110

BRIDGETTE OR JASON GAVRAS
38472 AVERY LANE
DALLAS, TX 75259

May 16 19 ___

PAY TO THE
ORDER OF _____   $ 1,483.21

_Fourteen hundred eighty-three 21/100_ DOLLARS

FOR CLASSROOM USE ONLY

**Midtown Bank**
Dallas, Texas

FOR _____

⑈11 10000 20⑈0729⑈ 578 1953⑈

---

V-16   0938

362-6/1119

UNITED RETIREMENT FUND
38273 RICHARDSON DRIVE
RICHARDSON, TX 75080

May 16 19 ___

PAY TO THE
ORDER OF _Terrill Investments_   $ 3,675.14

_Thirty-six hundred seventy-five and 14/100_ DOLLARS

**1** BANK AND TRUST
RICHARDSON • TEXAS

FOR CLASSROOM USE ONLY

FOR _____

⑈11900069⑈0938⑈ 147904 2⑈

_Olivia Redney_

---

## REQUEST FOR CUSTOMER INFORMATION  V-16

**Name** _____

**Acct. No.** _____

**Acct. Type** _____

**Last Deposit** _____

**Comments** _____

Please List Each Check Separately

| CHECKS | DOLLARS | CENTS |
|---|---|---|
| 1 Matson | 142 | 19 |
| 2 Bledsoe | 2,015 | 68 |
| 3 Talkington | 58 | 49 |
| 4 Jordan | 139 | 65 |
| 5 Lassiter | 76 | 15 |
| 6 | | |
| 7 | | |
| 8 | | |
| 9 | | |
| 10 | | |
| 11 | | |
| 12 | | |
| 13 | | |
| 14 | | |
| 15 | | |
| 16 | | |
| **TOTAL THIS SIDE** ENTER THIS TOTAL ON REVERSE SIDE | 2,432 | 16 |

## SIMULATED CASH FOR DISBURSEMENT

**Currency:**

| | |
|---|---|
| Hundreds | $ |
| Fifties | $ |
| Twenties | $ |
| Tens | $ |
| Fives | $ |
| Ones | $ |

**Total Currency** $

**Coins:**

| | |
|---|---|
| Dollars | $ |
| Halves | $ |
| Quarters | $ |
| Dimes | $ |
| Nickels | $ |
| Pennies | $ |

**Total Coins** $

**TOTAL CASH DISBURSED** $

(To Customer)

---

## SIMULATED CASH FOR DISBURSEMENT

**Currency:**

| | |
|---|---|
| Hundreds | $ |
| Fifties | $ |
| Twenties | $ |
| Tens | $ |
| Fives | $ |
| Ones | $ |

**Total Currency** $

**Coins:**

| | |
|---|---|
| Dollars | $ |
| Halves | $ |
| Quarters | $ |
| Dimes | $ |
| Nickels | $ |
| Pennies | $ |

**Total Coins** $

**TOTAL CASH DISBURSED** $

(To Customer)

---

## SIMULATED CASH FOR DISBURSEMENT

**Currency:**

| | |
|---|---|
| Hundreds | $ |
| Fifties | $ |
| Twenties | $ |
| Tens | $ |
| Fives | $ |
| Ones | $ |

**Total Currency** $

**Coins:**

| | |
|---|---|
| Dollars | $ |
| Halves | $ |
| Quarters | $ |
| Dimes | $ |
| Nickels | $ |
| Pennies | $ |

**Total Coins** $

**TOTAL CASH DISBURSED** $

(To Customer)

---

## SIMULATED CASH RECEIVED

**Currency:**

| | |
|---|---|
| Hundreds | $ |
| Fifties | $ |
| Twenties | $ |
| Tens | $ |
| Fives | $ |
| Ones | $ |

**Total Currency** $

**Coins:**

| | |
|---|---|
| Dollars | $ |
| Halves | $ |
| Quarters | $ |
| Dimes | $ |
| Nickels | $ |
| Pennies | $ |

**Total Coins** $

**TOTAL CASH RECEIVED** $

(To Teller Drawer)

---

## SIMULATED CASH RECEIVED

**Currency:**

| | | |
|---|---|---|
| 1 | Hundreds | $ 100.00 |
| 1 | Fifties | $ 50.00 |
| 25 | Twenties | $ 500.00 |
| 13 | Tens | $ 130.00 |
| 28 | Fives | $ 140.00 |
| 76 | Ones | $ 76.00 |

**Total Currency** $ 996.00

**Coins:**

| | | |
|---|---|---|
| | Dollars | $ |
| 7 | Halves | $ 3.50 |
| 2 rolls | Quarters | $ 20.00 |
| 3 rolls | Dimes | $ 15.00 |
| 5 rolls | Nickels | $ 10.00 |
| 1 rolls | Pennies | $ 3.50 |

**Total Coins** $ 52.00

**TOTAL CASH RECEIVED** $ 1,048.00

(To Teller Drawer)

**3102** (V-18)

GERANIUM HOUSE APARTMENTS
8765 E. BERKSHIRE LANE
DALLAS, TX 75248

32-1076/1110

May 16 19 —

PAY TO THE ORDER OF _C. Tyler Monroe Enterprises_ $1,086.51

One thousand eighty-six and 51/100 _____ DOLLARS

**S**ECURITY **FIRST BANK**
DALLAS, TEXAS

M.A. Mallory

FOR _____

⑈⑈⑉⑈⑆⑎⑊⑉⑇⑉⑊⑈⑊⑆⑅⑈⑉⑌⑆⑈⑅⑆⑋⑊⑆⑆⑊⑈⑆⑆⑈

---

**3194** (V-18)

LOPEZ CAR REPAIR
6432 HARTDALE
DALLAS, TEXAS 75211

32-29/1110

May 15 19 —

PAY TO THE ORDER OF _C. Tyler Monroe Enterprises_ $17.68

Seventeen and 68/100 _____ DOLLARS

**CNB** COMMUNITY
NATIONAL BANK
Dallas, Texas

Juanita Rogers

FOR _Dens. 1234_

⑈⑈⑉⑈⑆⑆⑆⑆⑊⑌⑊⑈⑉⑉⑈⑄⑋⑌⑈⑊⑉⑅⑇⑋⑍⑆⑊⑊⑇

---

**2178** (V-18)

HIRSCHFIELD PROTECTION SERVICES
43276 ILLINOIS
DALLAS, TX 75211

32-2/1110

May 11 19 —

PAY TO THE ORDER OF _C. Tyler Monroe_ $67.91

Sixty-seven and 91/100 _____ DOLLARS

**Midtown Bank**
Dallas, Texas

J.B. Hirschfield

FOR _m. acct._

⑈⑈⑉⑈⑆⑆⑆⑆⑆⑊⑈⑆⑊⑉⑉⑈⑊⑉⑇⑋⑌⑆⑈⑆⑋⑋⑊⑋⑌⑅⑊⑉

---

**0497** (V-18)

TALKINGTON TEMPORARIES
87654 DELRAY DRIVE
DALLAS, TEXAS 75043

32-76/1110

May 12 19 —

PAY TO THE ORDER OF _C. Tyler Monroe Enterprises_ $58.49

Fifty-eight and 49/100 _____ DOLLARS

_Northside State Bank_
Dallas, Texas

Jack Talkington

FOR _Acct. 631-468_

⑈⑈⑉⑈⑆⑆⑆⑆⑊⑌⑈⑉⑆⑌⑈⑊⑇⑋⑌⑅⑌⑊⑉⑆⑋⑉⑆⑈⑌

---

**0586** (V-18)

JORDAN BONDING COMPANY
7765 E. FOREST LANE
DALLAS, TEXAS 75234

32-866/1110

May 15 19 —

PAY TO THE ORDER OF _C. Tyler Monroe Enterprises_ $139.65

One hundred thirty-nine and 65/100 _____ DOLLARS

**D**ALLAS **C**OUNTY
**C**REDIT **U**NION __ Dallas, Texas

Mercy Jordan

FOR _____

⑈⑈⑉⑈⑆⑆⑆⑌⑌⑌⑆⑈⑊⑌⑉⑌⑌⑆⑆⑋⑍⑈⑉⑌⑋⑌⑌⑌

---

**4912** (V-18)

_Executive Cleaners_
87643 Addison Rd., Suite 69
Addison, Texas 75225

192-41/1119

May 14 19 —

PAY TO THE ORDER OF _C. Tyler Monroe Enterprises_ $76.15

Seventy-six and 15/100 _____ DOLLARS

**Addison Bank**
Addison, Texas

Leeman Loraster

MEMO _Inv. 51654_

⑈⑈⑉⑈⑌⑌⑆⑈⑆⑌⑉⑉⑊⑈⑉⑇⑇⑈⑌⑆⑇⑋⑌⑉⑌

## Check 16438 (V-19)

ELECTROSYSTEMS
46273 MILLER AVENUE
DALLAS, TEXAS 75205

32-29/1110

May 8 19 —

PAY TO THE ORDER OF _Ratliff Carpets_ $5,094.18

_Five thousand ninety-four and 18/100_ DOLLARS

**CNB** COMMUNITY
NATIONAL BANK
Dallas, Texas

FOR CLASSROOM USE ONLY

FOR _inv. 694348_          J. Randall Overton

⑈1110000 29⑈:⑈6438⑈⑈38 293 6475⑈

---

## Check 1373 (V-19)

Annette Kreck
2256 Holland Avenue
Dallas, Texas 75219

32-2571/1110

May 10 19 —

PAY TO THE ORDER OF _Ratliff Carpets_ $220.76

_Two hundred twenty and 76/100_ DOLLARS

**Dallas County Bank**
Dallas, Texas

FOR CLASSROOM USE ONLY

FOR _inv. 461384_          Annette Kreck

⑈1110 25710⑈:⑈1373⑈⑈6456 27⑈

---

## Check 1498 (V-19)

Robert Mozisek
78443 Peyton Drive
Dallas, Texas 75240

192-41/119

May 12 19 —

PAY TO THE ORDER OF _Ratliff Carpets_ $16.91

_Sixteen and 91/100_ DOLLARS

**Addison Bank**
Addison, Texas

FOR CLASSROOM USE ONLY

MEMO          Robert Mozisek

⑈111900418⑈:⑈1498⑈⑈6351859⑈

---

## Check 5861 (V-18)

Matson Hardwood Floors
3217B Curtis Drive
Garland, TX 75002

67-20/1119

May 12 19 —

PAY TO THE ORDER OF _Monroe Enterprises_ $142.19

_One Hundred Forty-two and 19/100_ Dollars

**First Bank of Garland** Garland, Texas

FOR CLASSROOM USE ONLY

Memo          Billy Matson

⑈111900 209⑈:⑈5861⑈⑈56 2905 2⑈

---

## Check 69128 (V-18)

FAIRBANKS NURSING CARE
8654 EMERY STREET
DALLAS, TX 75215

32-3958/1110

May 15 19 —

PAY TO THE ORDER OF _C. Tyler Monroe Enterprises_ $2,015.68

_Two thousand and fifteen and 68/100_ DOLLARS

**Fair Park Bank**
Dallas, Texas

FOR CLASSROOM USE ONLY

FOR _acct 6194_          E. R. Bledsoe, Jr.

⑈1110395 86⑈:⑈69128⑈⑈6 21890043⑈

---

## Deposit Ticket (V-19)

RATLIFF CARPETS
6753 AVENUE K
DALLAS, TX 75050

32-2/1110

DATE _May 17_ 19 —

**DEPOSIT TICKET**

USE OTHER SIDE FOR
ADDITIONAL LISTING

BE SURE EACH ITEM IS
PROPERLY ENDORSED

| C A S H | CURRENCY | | |
|---|---|---|---|
| | COIN | | |
| CHECKS (LIST SINGLY) _Electrosystems_ | | 5,094 | 18 |
| _Keyes_ | | 948 | 15 |
| _Ferrini_ | | 306 | 59 |
| TOTAL from reverse side | | 725 | 63 |
| **TOTAL** | | | |
| LESS CASH RECEIVED | | | |
| **NET DEPOSIT** | | 7,074 | 55 |

FOR CLASSROOM USE ONLY

SIGN HERE FOR LESS CASH RECEIVED

**Midtown Bank**
Dallas, Texas

⑈1110000 20⑈:     ⑈563 4817⑈

Monroe Enterprises
For Deposit
# 486-982-3

Tyler Monroe Enterprises
For Deposit
# 486-982-3

Please List Each Check Separately

| CHECKS | | DOLLARS | CENTS |
|---|---|---|---|
| 1 | Svenson | 487 | 96 |
| 2 | Mozisek | 16 | 91 |
| 3 | Kreck | 220 | 76 |
| 4 | | | |
| 5 | | | |
| 6 | | | |
| 7 | | | |
| 8 | | | |
| 9 | | | |
| 10 | | | |
| 11 | | | |
| 12 | | | |
| 13 | | | |
| 14 | | | |
| 15 | | | |
| 16 | | | |
| TOTAL THIS SIDE ENTER THIS TOTAL ON REVERSE SIDE | | 725 | 63 |

Ratliff Carpets

Ratliff Carpets

## Deposit Ticket

**SCOTT K. OR MARY JO NILSSON**
6423 MONETT STREET
DALLAS, TX 75204

32-2/1110

**DEPOSIT TICKET**
USE OTHER SIDE FOR
ADDITIONAL LISTING

BE SURE EACH ITEM IS
PROPERLY ENDORSED

| | C CURRENCY | |
|---|---|---|
| A | COIN | |
| S | H | |
| CHECKS (LIST SINGLY) | | |

| CHECKS (LIST SINGLY) | | |
|---|---|---|
| date | 365 | 00 |
| theater | 1,000 | 00 |
| Mercado | 1,386 | 52 |
| TOTAL from reverse side | | |
| **TOTAL** | 2,751 | 52 |
| LESS CASH RECEIVED | 150 | — |
| **NET DEPOSIT** | 2,601 | 52 |

DATE 5/17 19 —

SIGN HERE FOR LESS CASH RECEIVED

**Midtown Bank**
Dallas, Texas

⑈1⑈10000 20⑈   ⑈⑈4⑆6⑈8⑈9⑈3⑈2⑈'

---

**ROSE OR ALBERTO FERRINI**
4330 WOODCHIME COURT
DALLAS, TEXAS 75050

0842   V-19

32-29/1110

May 14 19 —

PAY TO THE
ORDER OF  Ratliff Carpets   $306.59

Three hundred six and 59/100 ——————— DOLLARS

**CNB COMMUNITY
NATIONAL BANK**
Dallas, Texas

FOR  L. A. carpet    Rose Ferrini

⑈1⑈10000 29⑈:08⑈4 2⑈46⑈77⑈2⑈78⑈19⑈'

---

**MARVIN SHARP OR PHYLLIS SHARP**
9862 ALHAMBRA
DALLAS, TX 75217

1628   V-20

32-2/1110

May 15 19 —

PAY TO THE
ORDER OF  Me   $365.00

Three hundred sixty-five and 00/100 ——— DOLLARS

**Midtown Bank**
Dallas, Texas

FOR          Phyllis Sharp

⑈1⑈10000 20⑈:16 28⑈57 28590⑈'

---

**GILBERT REYES, M.D.**
35467 BELT LINE RD., SUITE 35
DALLAS, TX 75081

4863   V-19

32-534/1110

May 16 19 —

PAY TO THE
ORDER OF  Ratliff Carpets   $948.15

Nine hundred forty-eight and 15/100 ———— DOLLARS

**DALLAS BANK**
DALLAS, TEXAS

FOR Inv: 461392    Gilbert Reyes

⑈1⑈1005⑈34⑈:⑈4⑈863⑈57⑈13⑈24⑈56⑈'

---

**Gaston Real Estate Management**
38293 Glen Lea Drive
Irving, TX 75063

2843   V-20

83-1010/1119

May 14 19 —

PAY TO THE
ORDER OF  Scott or Mary Jo Nilsson   $1,000.00

One thousand and 00/100 —————— DOLLARS

**Irving Savings**   Irving, Texas

MEMO

⑈1⑈1910103⑈:2843⑈35⑈2 278⑈59⑈'

Ella Easton

---

**TINY TOTS NURSERY**
674 TORONTO STREET
DALLAS, TX 75212

1356   V-19

32-934/1110

May 15 19 —

PAY TO THE
ORDER OF  Ratliff Carpets   $487.96

Four hundred eighty-seven and 96/100 —DOLLARS

**Dallas METROPLEX Bank**
Dallas, Texas

FOR Paint. 69 4 3 46

Eileen Sorensen

⑈1⑈100934⑈:⑈1356⑈276⑈34⑈985⑈'

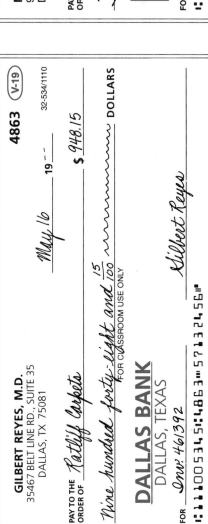
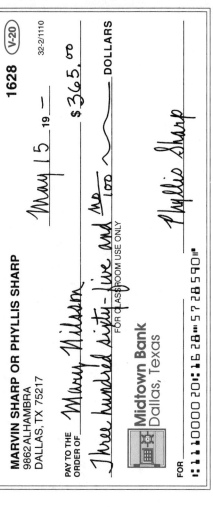

*Scott Nielson*
*For deposit*

*Mary Wilson*
*For deposit*

Please List Each Check Separately

| CHECKS | DOLLARS | CENTS |
|--------|---------|-------|
| 1 | | |
| 2 | | |
| 3 | | |
| 4 | | |
| 5 | | |
| 6 | | |
| 7 | | |
| 8 | | |
| 9 | | |
| 10 | | |
| 11 | | |
| 12 | | |
| 13 | | |
| 14 | | |
| 15 | | |
| 16 | | |
| TOTAL THIS SIDE ENTER THIS TOTAL ON REVERSE SIDE | | |

*Ratliff carpets*

*Ratliff carpets*

*Ratliff carpets*

## Check V-20

**MERCEDES INSURANCE AGENCY**
57348 RAINIER
IRVING, TEXAS 75063

No. 3866
83-51/1119

May 16 19 __

PAY TO THE ORDER OF _Scott and Mary Jo Nilson_ $1,386.52

_Thirteen hundred eighty-six and 52/100_ DOLLARS

**IRVING BANK**
IRVING, TEXAS

FOR CLASSROOM USE ONLY

FOR _____

R. J. Mercedes

⑈119005⑈0⑈3866⑈ 1953759 24⑈

---

## Deposit Ticket V-21

**DEPOSIT TICKET**
USE OTHER SIDE FOR ADDITIONAL LISTING

BE SURE EACH ITEM IS PROPERLY ENDORSED

32-2/1110

| | | |
|---|---|---|
| CURRENCY | | |
| COIN | | |
| CHECKS (LIST SINGLY) | | |
| Walker | 648 | 93 |
| TOTAL from reverse side | | |
| **TOTAL** | 648 | 93 |
| LESS CASH RECEIVED | 100 | — |
| **NET DEPOSIT** | 548 | 93 |

PATRICK F. OR
FRANCES E. O'SULLIVAN
13123 CLEARCREST DR.
DALLAS, TX 75002

DATE 5-17 19 __

SIGN HERE FOR LESS CASH RECEIVED

**Midtown Bank**
Dallas, Texas

⑈110000 20⑈ "586391 2⑈"

---

## Check V-21

**WALKER BROTHERS & ASSOCIATES**
5437 RED BIRD LANE
DALLAS, TX 75237

No. 2981
32-69/1110

May 15 19 __

PAY TO THE ORDER OF _Frances E. O'Sullivan_ $648.93

_Six hundred forty-eight and 93/100_ DOLLARS

**Southside Bank**
Dallas, Texas

FOR CLASSROOM USE ONLY

FOR _____

Alvin R. Walker

⑈110006⑈ 9⑈ 298 ⑈ 5633986 54⑈

---

## Transaction Request Form

### TRANSACTION REQUEST FORM

V-21

**Midtown Bank**
Dallas, Texas

**Name** Frances E. O'Sullivan      **Date** _____

**Account #** 586-391-3      **Teller** _____

**DEPOSIT**  Acct. Type: Checking ☐  Savings ☐

| | | |
|---|---|---|
| Cash | | |
| Checks | _____ | |
| | _____ | |
| | _____ | |
| | _____ | |
| | _____ | |
| Total Received | | |
| Less Cash Received | | |
| Net Deposit | | |

**WITHDRAWAL**

Checking   $_____
Savings    $_____

**TRANSFER**

$_____
From Acct. # _____
To Acct. # _____

**Signature** _____

Please List Each Check Separately

| CHECKS | DOLLARS | CENTS |
|---|---|---|
| 1 | | |
| 2 | | |
| 3 | | |
| 4 | | |
| 5 | | |
| 6 | | |
| 7 | | |
| 8 | | |
| 9 | | |
| 10 | | |
| 11 | | |
| 12 | | |
| 13 | | |
| 14 | | |
| 15 | | |
| 16 | | |
| **TOTAL THIS SIDE** ENTER THIS TOTAL ON REVERSE SIDE | | |

# TALLY SHEET

VI

DATE _____

| (1) $ Denominations | (2) Total Cash Brought Forward | (3) Transactions  + or – | | | | | | | | | | | | | | | | | | | | (4) = Total $ |
|---|---|---|---|---|---|---|---|---|---|---|---|---|---|---|---|---|---|---|---|---|---|---|
| **BILLS:** Hundreds  $100 | 2,000 | | | | | | | | | | | | | | | | | | | | | |
| Fifties  $50 | 200 | | | | | | | | | | | | | | | | | | | | | |
| Twenties  $20 | 1,700 | | | | | | | | | | | | | | | | | | | | | |
| Tens  $10 | 500 | | | | | | | | | | | | | | | | | | | | | |
| Fives  $5 | 250 | | | | | | | | | | | | | | | | | | | | | |
| Ones  $1 | 225 | | | | | | | | | | | | | | | | | | | | | |
| **COINS:** Dollars  $1 | 5 | | | | | | | | | | | | | | | | | | | | | |
| Halves  .50 | 16 | | | | | | | | | | | | | | | | | | | | | |
| Quarters  .25 | 50 | | | | | | | | | | | | | | | | | | | | | |
| Dimes  .10 | 35 | | | | | | | | | | | | | | | | | | | | | |
| Nickels  .05 | 15 | | | | | | | | | | | | | | | | | | | | | |
| Pennies  .01 | 4 | | | | | | | | | | | | | | | | | | | | | |
| | 5,000 | | | | | | | | | | | | | | | | | | | | | |

(5) Total Cash

(6) Minus (–) Amount Transferred to Vault Account at Closing

(7) Cash Brought Forward

## Check 7632 (VI-1)

MR. OR MRS. DOUGLAS FORWICK
4756 HUNTERS GLEN
DALLAS, TX 75150

7632
48-38/1119

May 16 19—

PAY TO THE ORDER OF _Anderson Brick Products, Inc._ $ 1,026.54

_One thousand twenty-six and 54/100_ DOLLARS

Second Bank of Plano
PLANO, TEXAS

FOR _Inv. 60184_

Douglas Forwick

⑈1119003 85⑈763 ⑈5738 219⑈

---

## Deposit Ticket (VI-1)

ANDERSON BRICK PRODUCTS, INC.
7122 GLENCOE
DALLAS, TX 75206

DEPOSIT TICKET
32-2/1110

USE OTHER SIDE FOR ADDITIONAL LISTING

BE SURE EACH ITEM IS PROPERLY ENDORSED

DATE May 18 19 — —

| CASH | CURRENCY | | |
|---|---|---|---|
| | COIN | | |
| CHECKS (LIST SINGLY) | | | |
| 7632 | | 1,026 | 54 |
| 0955 | | 864 | 35 |
| TOTAL from reverse side | | 1,209 | 13 |
| | | 3,100 | 02 |
| TOTAL | | 3,100 | 02 |
| LESS CASH RECEIVED | | | |
| NET DEPOSIT | | | |

FOR CLASSROOM USE ONLY

SIGN HERE FOR LESS CASH RECEIVED

Midtown Bank
Dallas, Texas

⑈110000 20⑈ ⑈6879435⑈

---

## Check 7622 (VI-2)

HENRY R. KIRTON
51968 HAINES AVENUE
DALLAS, TX 75208

7622
32-2/1110

May 18 19 —

PAY TO THE ORDER OF _Midtown Bank_ $ 150.00

_One hundred fifty and no/100_ DOLLARS

Midtown Bank
Dallas, Texas

FOR

Henry R. Kirton

⑈110000 20⑈76 2 ⑈387968⑈

---

## Check 8341 (VI-1)

JESSICA OR RONALD R. HUGHEY
2436 KIMBALDALE
DALLAS, TX 75233

8341
32-11/1110

May 10 19 —

PAY TO THE ORDER OF _Anderson Brick Products_ $ 265.86

_Two hundred sixty-five and 86/100_ DOLLARS

NORTHSIDE FEDERAL BANK
DALLAS TEXAS

FOR CLASSROOM USE ONLY

FOR

Jessica Hughey

⑈110003 2⑈834 ⑈6894 288⑈

---

## Check 0682 (VI-1)

Edwin R. Goodlett
3647 Abramshire
Dallas, TX 75231

0682
83-1010/1119

May 13 19 — —

PAY TO THE ORDER OF _Anderson Brick Products_ $ 943.27

_Nine hundred forty-three and 27/100_ DOLLARS

Irving Savings  Irving, Texas

FOR CLASSROOM USE ONLY

MEMO

Edwin R. Goodlett

⑈1119010 103⑈068 2⑈38 2749 83⑈

---

## Check 0955 (VI-1)

Miracle Optical, Inc.
3829 Addington
Addison, Texas 75225

0955
192-41/1119

May 15 19 — —

PAY TO THE ORDER OF _Anderson Brick Products, Inc._ $ 864.35

_Eight hundred sixty-four and 35/100_ DOLLARS

Addison Bank
Addison, Texas

FOR CLASSROOM USE ONLY

MEMO _Inv. 60166_

Janice Johnson

⑈1190041⑈0955 ⑈728 3746⑈

**ENDORSE HERE**

For Deposit

Anderson Brick Products

**DO NOT WRITE, STAMP OR SIGN BELOW THIS LINE**
RESERVED FOR FINANCIAL INSTITUTION USE'

---

Please List Each Check Separately

| CHECKS | DOLLARS | CENTS |
| --- | --- | --- |
| 1 | 8341 | 265 | 86 |
| 2 | 682 | 943 | 27 |
| 3 | | | |
| 4 | | | |
| 5 | | | |
| 6 | | | |
| 7 | | | |
| 8 | | | |
| 9 | | | |
| 10 | | | |
| 11 | | | |
| 12 | | | |
| 13 | | | |
| 14 | | | |
| 15 | | | |
| 16 | | | |
| TOTAL THIS SIDE — ENTER THIS TOTAL ON REVERSE SIDE | 1,209 | 13 |

**ENDORSE HERE**

**DO NOT WRITE, STAMP OR SIGN BELOW THIS LINE**
RESERVED FOR FINANCIAL INSTITUTION USE'

---

**ENDORSE HERE**

For Deposit

Anderson Brick Products

**DO NOT WRITE, STAMP OR SIGN BELOW THIS LINE**
RESERVED FOR FINANCIAL INSTITUTION USE'

---

**DO NOT WRITE, STAMP OR SIGN BELOW THIS LINE**
RESERVED FOR FINANCIAL INSTITUTION USE'

For Deposit

Anderson Brick Products

**ENDORSE HERE**

---

**DO NOT WRITE, STAMP OR SIGN BELOW THIS LINE**
RESERVED FOR FINANCIAL INSTITUTION USE'

For Deposit

Anderson Brick Products

**ENDORSE HERE**

---

**DO NOT WRITE, STAMP OR SIGN BELOW THIS LINE**
RESERVED FOR FINANCIAL INSTITUTION USE'

For Deposit

Anderson Brick Products

**ENDORSE HERE**

## SIMULATED CASH FOR DISBURSEMENT

Currency:

| | | |
|---|---|---|
| ____ | Hundreds | $ ____ |
| ____ | Fifties | $ ____ |
| ____ | Twenties | $ ____ |
| ____ | Tens | $ ____ |
| ____ | Fives | $ ____ |
| ____ | Ones | $ ____ |

Total Currency $ ____

Coins:

| | | |
|---|---|---|
| ____ | Dollars | $ ____ |
| ____ | Halves | $ ____ |
| ____ | Quarters | $ ____ |
| ____ | Dimes | $ ____ |
| ____ | Nickels | $ ____ |
| ____ | Pennies | $ ____ |

Total Coins $ ____

TOTAL CASH DISBURSED $ ____

(To Customer)

## SIMULATED CASH RECEIVED

Currency:

| | | |
|---|---|---|
| ____ | Hundreds | $ ____ |
| 1 | Fifties | $ 50.00 |
| 3 | Twenties | $ 60.00 |
| 5 | Tens | $ 50.00 |
| 18 | Fives | $ 90.00 |
| 36 | Ones | $ 36.00 |

Total Currency $ 286.00

Coins:

| | | |
|---|---|---|
| ____ | Dollars | $ ____ |
| ____ | Halves | $ ____ |
| 45 | Quarters | $ 11.25 |
| 30 | Dimes | $ 3.00 |
| 18 | Nickels | $ .90 |
| 76 | Pennies | $ .76 |

Total Coins $ 15.91

TOTAL CASH RECEIVED $ 301.91

(To Teller Drawer)

## SIMULATED CASH FOR DISBURSEMENT

Currency:

| | | |
|---|---|---|
| ____ | Hundreds | $ ____ |
| ____ | Fifties | $ ____ |
| ____ | Twenties | $ ____ |
| ____ | Tens | $ ____ |
| ____ | Fives | $ ____ |
| ____ | Ones | $ ____ |

Total Currency $ ____

Coins:

| | | |
|---|---|---|
| ____ | Dollars | $ ____ |
| ____ | Halves | $ ____ |
| ____ | Quarters | $ ____ |
| ____ | Dimes | $ ____ |
| ____ | Nickels | $ ____ |
| ____ | Pennies | $ ____ |

Total Coins $ ____

TOTAL CASH DISBURSED $ ____

(To Customer)

## SIMULATED CASH FOR DISBURSEMENT

Currency:

| | | |
|---|---|---|
| ____ | Hundreds | $ ____ |
| ____ | Fifties | $ ____ |
| ____ | Twenties | $ ____ |
| ____ | Tens | $ ____ |
| ____ | Fives | $ ____ |
| ____ | Ones | $ ____ |

Total Currency $ ____

Coins:

| | | |
|---|---|---|
| ____ | Dollars | $ ____ |
| ____ | Halves | $ ____ |
| ____ | Quarters | $ ____ |
| ____ | Dimes | $ ____ |
| ____ | Nickels | $ ____ |
| ____ | Pennies | $ ____ |

Total Coins $ ____

TOTAL CASH DISBURSED $ ____

(To Customer)

## SIMULATED CASH FOR DISBURSEMENT

Currency:

| | | |
|---|---|---|
| ____ | Hundreds | $ ____ |
| ____ | Fifties | $ ____ |
| ____ | Twenties | $ ____ |
| ____ | Tens | $ ____ |
| ____ | Fives | $ ____ |
| ____ | Ones | $ ____ |

Total Currency $ ____

Coins:

| | | |
|---|---|---|
| ____ | Dollars | $ ____ |
| ____ | Halves | $ ____ |
| ____ | Quarters | $ ____ |
| ____ | Dimes | $ ____ |
| ____ | Nickels | $ ____ |
| ____ | Pennies | $ ____ |

Total Coins $ ____

TOTAL CASH DISBURSED $ ____

(To Customer)

## SIMULATED CASH FOR DISBURSEMENT

Currency:

| | | |
|---|---|---|
| ____ | Hundreds | $ ____ |
| ____ | Fifties | $ ____ |
| ____ | Twenties | $ ____ |
| ____ | Tens | $ ____ |
| ____ | Fives | $ ____ |
| ____ | Ones | $ ____ |

Total Currency $ ____

Coins:

| | | |
|---|---|---|
| ____ | Dollars | $ ____ |
| ____ | Halves | $ ____ |
| ____ | Quarters | $ ____ |
| ____ | Dimes | $ ____ |
| ____ | Nickels | $ ____ |
| ____ | Pennies | $ ____ |

Total Coins $ ____

TOTAL CASH DISBURSED $ ____

(To Customer)

## Check 1211 — VI-4

**SHEILA R. CRADDUCK**
4436 IDLEWILD
DALLAS, TX 75050

No. 1211
32-11/1110

May 10 19 —

PAY TO THE ORDER OF _George T. Lucas, Esq._  $250 00

Two hundred fifty and no/100 _____ DOLLARS

NORTHSIDE FEDERAL BANK
DALLAS, TEXAS

FOR _____

Sheila R. Cradduck

⑆1110003 26⑆ 1 26⑈ 574 98 2098⑈

## Check 2311 — VI-4

**MARIO ORTIZ**
844 SYCAMORE STREET
DALLAS, TEXAS 75115

No. 2311
32-29/1110

5/12 19 —

PAY TO THE ORDER OF _George T. Lucas, Esq._  $790.00

Seven hundred ninety and no/100 _____ DOLLARS

CNB COMMUNITY NATIONAL BANK
Dallas, Texas

FOR _Fees to Ortiz_

Mario Ortiz

⑆1110000 29⑆ 2311⑈ 4 736 2906⑈

## Check 78115 — VI-4

**Mesquite Employment Agency**
47328 First Avenue
Mesquite, Texas 75029

No. 78115
392-95/1119

May 13 19 —

PAY TO THE ORDER OF _George T. Lucas, Esq._  $500.00

Five hundred and no/100 _____ DOLLARS

**Greater Mesquite Bank**
Mesquite • Texas

FOR _On act._

Arthur O'Toole

⑆11900 59⑆ 78115⑈ 68 584 73⑈

## Deposit Ticket — VI-3

**PHYLIS A. OR R. T. LEE**
8513 WESTMINSTER
DALLAS, TX 75205

32-2/1110

DATE May 18 19 —

| | CURRENCY | | |
|---|---|---|---|
| C A S H | COIN | | |
| CHECKS (LIST SINGLY) | | | |
| | Bunch | 286 | 51 |
| TOTAL from reverse side | | | |
| **TOTAL** | | 286 | 51 |
| LESS CASH RECEIVED | | 17 | 00 |
| **NET DEPOSIT** | | 269 | 51 |

SIGN HERE FOR LESS CASH RECEIVED _____

FOR CLASSROOM USE ONLY

DEPOSIT TICKET
USE OTHER SIDE FOR ADDITIONAL LISTING

BE SURE EACH ITEM IS PROPERLY ENDORSED

**Midtown Bank**
Dallas, Texas

⑆1110000 20⑆ ⑈5689 3 24⑈

## Check 9083 — VI-3

**BUNCH MOVIE RENTALS**
4738 EDGEWOOD DRIVE
DALLAS, TX 75211

No. 9083
32-934/1110

May 13 19 —

PAY TO THE ORDER OF _Phyllis Lee_  $286.51

Two hundred eighty-six and 51/100 _____ DOLLARS

**Dallas METROPLEX Bank**
Dallas, Texas

FOR _____

Oscar Bunch

FOR CLASSROOM USE ONLY

⑆110093 45⑆ 9083⑈ 4 736 25390⑈

## Deposit Ticket — VI-4

**GEORGE T. LUCAS, ESQ.**
708 PARK LANE
DALLAS, TX 75223

32-2/1110

DATE May 18 19 —

| | CURRENCY | | |
|---|---|---|---|
| C A S H | COIN | | |
| CHECKS (LIST SINGLY) | | | |
| | Cradduck | 250 | — |
| | Johnson | 525 | — |
| | Batson | 420 | — |
| TOTAL from reverse side | | 3,471 | 51 |
| **TOTAL** | | 4,666 | 51 |
| LESS CASH RECEIVED | | | |
| **NET DEPOSIT** | | 4,666 | 51 |

SIGN HERE FOR LESS CASH RECEIVED _____

FOR CLASSROOM USE ONLY

DEPOSIT TICKET
USE OTHER SIDE FOR ADDITIONAL LISTING

BE SURE EACH ITEM IS PROPERLY ENDORSED

**Midtown Bank**
Dallas, Texas

⑆1110000 20⑆ ⑈3869 5 12⑈

Please List Each Check Separately

| CHECKS | DOLLARS | CENTS |
|---|---|---|
| 1 | | |
| 2 | | |
| 3 | | |
| 4 | | |
| 5 | | |
| 6 | | |
| 7 | | |
| 8 | | |
| 9 | | |
| 10 | | |
| 11 | | |
| 12 | | |
| 13 | | |
| 14 | | |
| 15 | | |
| 16 | | |
| **TOTAL THIS SIDE** ENTER THIS TOTAL ON REVERSE SIDE | | |

**ENDORSE HERE**

**DO NOT WRITE, STAMP OR SIGN BELOW THIS LINE**
RESERVED FOR FINANCIAL INSTITUTION USE*

*FEDERAL RESERVE BOARD OF GOVERNORS REG. CC

Please List Each Check Separately

| CHECKS | DOLLARS | CENTS |
|---|---|---|
| 1 Mesquite | 500 | — |
| 2 Ortiz | 790 | — |
| 3 Linn | 210 | — |
| 4 Limon | 1,027 | 65 |
| 5 Dupree | 943 | 86 |
| 6 | | |
| 7 | | |
| 8 | | |
| 9 | | |
| 10 | | |
| 11 | | |
| 12 | | |
| 13 | | |
| 14 | | |
| 15 | | |
| 16 | | |
| **TOTAL THIS SIDE** ENTER THIS TOTAL ON REVERSE SIDE | 3,471 | 51 |

**ENDORSE HERE**

George T. Lucas, Esq.

**DO NOT WRITE, STAMP OR SIGN BELOW THIS LINE**
RESERVED FOR FINANCIAL INSTITUTION USE*

*FEDERAL RESERVE BOARD OF GOVERNORS REG. CC

**ENDORSE HERE**

George T. Lucas, Esq.

**DO NOT WRITE, STAMP OR SIGN BELOW THIS LINE**
RESERVED FOR FINANCIAL INSTITUTION USE*

*FEDERAL RESERVE BOARD OF GOVERNORS REG. CC

**ENDORSE HERE**

George T. Lucas, Esq.

**DO NOT WRITE, STAMP OR SIGN BELOW THIS LINE**
RESERVED FOR FINANCIAL INSTITUTION USE*

*FEDERAL RESERVE BOARD OF GOVERNORS REG. CC

R. J. OR MARTHA JOHNSON
3411 MENTON AVENUE
DALLAS, TX 75216

5114  VI-4

32-69/1110

May 15  19 --

PAY TO THE ORDER OF  George T. Lucas, Esq.  $ 525.00

Five Hundred Twenty-five and 00/100 ——————— DOLLARS

**S**outhside Bank
Dallas, Texas

FOR CLASSROOM USE ONLY

R. J. Johnson

FOR _____

⑆1100069⑆ 5114 ⑈ 576633218⑈

---

PLANO READING LAB
57348 PARK
PLANO, TX 75074

7833  VI-4

48-38/1119

May 16  19 --

PAY TO THE ORDER OF  George T. Lucas, Esq.  $ 420.00

Four hundred twenty and no/100 ——————— DOLLARS

Second Bank of Plano
PLANO, TEXAS

FOR CLASSROOM USE ONLY

Patricia Batson

FOR _____

⑆1100385⑆ 7833 ⑈ 900611⑈

---

NANCY OR ROGER LIMON
54333 MORTON
DALLAS, TX 75211

0665  VI-4

32-3958/1110

May 13  19 --

PAY TO THE ORDER OF  George J. Lucas, Esq.  $ 1027.65

One thousand twenty-seven and 65/100 ——————— DOLLARS

Fair Park Bank
Dallas, Texas

FOR CLASSROOM USE ONLY

Roger Limon

FOR _____

⑆1103958⑆ 0665 ⑈ 3846 17400⑈

---

MR. OR MRS. DAVID DUPREE
57473 LAUDER LANE
DALLAS, TX 75248

3321  VI-4

32-1076/1110

May 14  19 --

PAY TO THE ORDER OF  George T. Lucas, Esq.  $ 943.86

Nine hundred forty-three and 86/100 ——————— DOLLARS

**S**ECURITY FIRST BANK
DALLAS, TEXAS

FOR CLASSROOM USE ONLY

Mrs. David Dupree

FOR _____

⑆1101076⑆ 332⑈ 5717 37 27⑈

---

Jinnifer and Richard Linn
65443 N. Bluegrove Rd.
Dallas, Texas 75134

7874  VI-4

192-41/1119

May 15  19 --

PAY TO THE ORDER OF  George T. Lucas, Esq.  $ 210.00

Two hundred ten and 00/100 ——————— DOLLARS

**Addison Bank**
Addison, Texas

MEMO  services

Richard Linn

Jinnifer Linn

FOR CLASSROOM USE ONLY

⑆1190048⑆ 7874 ⑈ 908 76 765⑈

---

**ENDORSE HERE**

George T. Lucas, Esq.

_____

_____

**DO NOT WRITE, STAMP OR SIGN BELOW THIS LINE**
RESERVED FOR FINANCIAL INSTITUTION USE*

*FEDERAL RESERVE BOARD OF GOVERNORS REG. CC

**ENDORSE HERE**

George T. Lucas, Esq.

_____

_____

**DO NOT WRITE, STAMP OR SIGN BELOW THIS LINE**
RESERVED FOR FINANCIAL INSTITUTION USE*

*FEDERAL RESERVE BOARD OF GOVERNORS REG. CC

**ENDORSE HERE**

George T. Lucas, Esq.

_____

_____

**DO NOT WRITE, STAMP OR SIGN BELOW THIS LINE**
RESERVED FOR FINANCIAL INSTITUTION USE*

*FEDERAL RESERVE BOARD OF GOVERNORS REG. CC

**ENDORSE HERE**

George T. Lucas, Esq.

_____

_____

**DO NOT WRITE, STAMP OR SIGN BELOW THIS LINE**
RESERVED FOR FINANCIAL INSTITUTION USE*

*FEDERAL RESERVE BOARD OF GOVERNORS REG. CC

**ENDORSE HERE**

George T. Lucas, Esq.

_____

_____

**DO NOT WRITE, STAMP OR SIGN BELOW THIS LINE**
RESERVED FOR FINANCIAL INSTITUTION USE*

*FEDERAL RESERVE BOARD OF GOVERNORS REG. CC

## Deposit Ticket (VI-7)

32-2/1110

GREGORY S. AND
JOYCE A. BRUCKER
5627 HIGHLAND OAKS
DALLAS, TX 75232

DATE _May 9_ 19 _--_

SIGN HERE FOR LESS CASH RECEIVED

**Midtown Bank**
Dallas, Texas

⑂:⑂⑂⑂0000 20⑂: ⑂⑂349589 6⑂⑂

| | CURRENCY | | |
|---|---|---|---|
| C A S H | COIN | | |
| CHECKS (LIST SINGLY) | | | |
| | Merriman | 694 | 31 |
| TOTAL from reverse side | | | |
| **TOTAL** | | 694 | 31 |
| LESS CASH RECEIVED | | | |
| **NET DEPOSIT** | | 694 | 31 |

**DEPOSIT TICKET**
USE OTHER SIDE FOR
ADDITIONAL LISTING

BE SURE EACH ITEM IS
PROPERLY ENDORSED

FOR CLASSROOM USE ONLY

---

## Check 7890 (VI-7)

7890

32-76/1110

ALEX J. MERRIMAN
6532 TOPHILL
DALLAS, TEXAS 75240

_May 12_ 19 _--_

$694.31

PAY TO THE
ORDER OF _Joyce Brucker_

_Six hundred ninety-four and 31/100_ ——— DOLLARS

_Northside State Bank_
Dallas, Texas

FOR _____

FOR CLASSROOM USE ONLY

_Alex J. Merriman_

⑂:⑂⑂⑂0000 768⑂:7890⑂⑂8374619 06⑂⑂

---

## Check 0987 (VI-8)

0987

32-1076/1110

LIONEL R. COZIER
5746 WINSTON
DALLAS, TX 75206

_May 12_ 19 _--_

$94.36

PAY TO THE
ORDER OF _Jacob J. Bowers_

_Ninety-four and 36/100_ ——— DOLLARS

**S**ECURITY FIRST BANK
DALLAS, TEXAS

FOR _____

FOR CLASSROOM USE ONLY

_Lionel R. Cozier_

⑂:⑂⑂⑂10 768⑂:098 7⑂⑂5648 234⑂⑂

---

## Check 68574631 (VI-5)

68574631

322-41/222

UNITED STATES GOVERNMENT
Washington, D.C.

May 15 19 _--_

$3,087.94

PAY TO THE
ORDER OF _A. R. Turner-Carr_

Three thousand eighty-seven & 94/100 ————————— DOLLARS

UNITED STATES
TREASURY DEPARTMENT
WASHINGTON, D.C.

681-493-5642

FOR _____

FOR CLASSROOM USE ONLY

⑂:222000 41⑂:6857463 1⑂574747 3⑂⑂

---

## Deposit Ticket (VI-5)

32-2/1110

A. R. TURNER-CARR
1534 MARSHALL DRIVE
DALLAS, TX 75240

DATE _May 18_ 19 _--_

SIGN HERE FOR LESS CASH RECEIVED

**Midtown Bank**
Dallas, Texas

⑂:⑂⑂⑂0000 20⑂: ⑂⑂684 93 25⑂⑂

| | CURRENCY | | |
|---|---|---|---|
| C A S H | COIN | | |
| CHECKS (LIST SINGLY) | | | |
| | 68574631 | 3,087 | 94 |
| TOTAL from reverse side | | | |
| **TOTAL** | | | |
| LESS CASH RECEIVED | | | |
| **NET DEPOSIT** | | 3,087 | 94 |

**DEPOSIT TICKET**
USE OTHER SIDE FOR
ADDITIONAL LISTING

BE SURE EACH ITEM IS
PROPERLY ENDORSED

FOR CLASSROOM USE ONLY

---

## Check 7866 (VI-6)

7866

32-76/1110

JONES CONSTRUCTION
57348 JOSEY LANE
CARROLTON, TEXAS 75056

_May 15_ 19 _--_

$550.00

PAY TO THE
ORDER OF _Albetto Guerrero_

_Five hundred fifty and no/100_ ——— DOLLARS

_Northside State Bank_
Dallas, Texas

FOR _____

FOR CLASSROOM USE ONLY

_Billy Jones_

⑂:⑂⑂⑂0000 768⑂:7866⑂⑂9088643 3 2⑂⑂

A. R. Turner – Carr

For deposit

Please List Each Check Separately

| CHECKS | DOLLARS | CENTS |
|---|---|---|
| 1 | | |
| 2 | | |
| 3 | | |
| 4 | | |
| 5 | | |
| 6 | | |
| 7 | | |
| 8 | | |
| 9 | | |
| 10 | | |
| 11 | | |
| 12 | | |
| 13 | | |
| 14 | | |
| 15 | | |
| 16 | | |
| TOTAL THIS SIDE ENTER THIS TOTAL ON REVERSE SIDE | | |

Please List Each Check Separately

| CHECKS | DOLLARS | CENTS |
|---|---|---|
| 1 | | |
| 2 | | |
| 3 | | |
| 4 | | |
| 5 | | |
| 6 | | |
| 7 | | |
| 8 | | |
| 9 | | |
| 10 | | |
| 11 | | |
| 12 | | |
| 13 | | |
| 14 | | |
| 15 | | |
| 16 | | |
| TOTAL THIS SIDE ENTER THIS TOTAL ON REVERSE SIDE | | |

Joyce Brucker
For deposit # 3695896

Jacob F. Bowers

## Deposit Ticket — Lella S. Petrosina

LELLA M. PETROSINA
1964 CRESTVIEW DR.
DALLAS, TX 75154

32-2/1110

DATE May 18 19 ___

SIGN HERE FOR LESS CASH RECEIVED
Lella S. Petrosina

**Midtown Bank**
Dallas, Texas

⑈⑈⑈⑈0000 20⑈    ⑈683481 5⑈⑈

| | CURRENCY | | |
|---|---|---|---|
| C A S H | COIN | | |
| | CHECKS (LIST SINGLY) | | |
| | Berens | 375 | 14 |
| | 1223 | 200 | 00 |
| | TOTAL from reverse side | | |
| | **TOTAL** | 575 | 14 |
| | LESS CASH RECEIVED | 200 | 00 |
| | **NET DEPOSIT** | 375 | 14 |

FOR CLASSROOM USE ONLY

---

## Check 1223 — Melody or R. D. Petrosina

1223
35-8477/1119

Melody or R. D. Petrosina
5621 Pine Ridge
Athens, TX 75751

May 5 19 ___

Pay to the Order of _____  $ 200.⁰⁰

Two hundred and 00/100 _____ DOLLARS

**ACB** Athens Center Bank
Athens, Texas

FOR CLASSROOM USE ONLY

Melody S. Petrosina

For _____

⑈⑈⑈1984771⑈ 1223⑈ 765389 2674⑈

---

## Check 13467 — Berens Heating & Cooling

13467
33-63/1119

Berens Heating & Cooling
3847 Camp Bowie
Fort Worth, Texas 75421

5 - 8 19 ___

PAY TO THE ORDER OF Lella Petrosina  $ 375.14

Three hundred seventy-five and 14/100 _____ DOLLARS

**Trinity River Savings**
Fort Worth, Texas

FOR CLASSROOM USE ONLY

FOR Refund _____  John Berens

⑈⑈⑈190063 8⑈ 3467⑈ 87644 23⑈

---

## Deposit Ticket — Carlos M. or Veronica Viviano

CARLOS M. OR
VERONICA VIVIANO
9995 RED BUD DRIVE
DALLAS, TX 75115

32-2/1110

DATE May 18 19 ___

SIGN HERE FOR LESS CASH RECEIVED

**Midtown Bank**
Dallas, Texas

⑈⑈⑈⑈0000 20⑈    ⑈9086435⑈⑈

| | CURRENCY | 286 | — |
|---|---|---|---|
| C A S H | COIN | 15 | 91 |
| | CHECKS (LIST SINGLY) | | |
| | TOTAL from reverse side | | |
| | **TOTAL** | 301 | 91 |
| | LESS CASH RECEIVED | | |
| | **NET DEPOSIT** | 301 | 91 |

FOR CLASSROOM USE ONLY

---

## Check 34512 — Graves Graphics Group

34512
25-322/1119

GRAVES GRAPHICS GROUP
38279 FIRST STREET
ARLINGTON, TX 75306

May 13 19 ___

PAY TO THE ORDER OF Daniel Jones  $ 1,608.94

Sixteen hundred eight and 94/100 _____ DOLLARS

**SECOND BANK OF ARLINGTON**
ARLINGTON, TEXAS

FOR CLASSROOM USE ONLY

MEMO _____  Marilyce Graves

⑈⑈⑈190328⑈ 34512⑈ 784637 28 7⑈⑈

---

## Deposit Ticket — Thomas J. Jones or Daniel W. Jones

THOMAS J. JONES OR
DANIEL W. JONES
3216 CARLISLE ST.
DALLAS, TX 75204

32-2/1110

DATE May 18 19 ___

SIGN HERE FOR LESS CASH RECEIVED

**Midtown Bank**
Dallas, Texas

⑈⑈⑈⑈0000 20⑈    ⑈591684 2⑈⑈

| | CURRENCY | | |
|---|---|---|---|
| C A S H | COIN | | |
| | CHECKS (LIST SINGLY) | | |
| | 34512 | 1,608 | 94 |
| | TOTAL from reverse side | | |
| | **TOTAL** | 1,608 | 94 |
| | LESS CASH RECEIVED | 58 | 94 |
| | **NET DEPOSIT** | 1,550 | 00 |

FOR CLASSROOM USE ONLY

DEPOSIT TICKET
USE OTHER SIDE FOR ADDITIONAL LISTING
BE SURE EACH ITEM IS PROPERLY ENDORSED

Please List Each Check Separately

| CHECKS | DOLLARS | CENTS |
|--------|---------|-------|
| 1 | | |
| 2 | | |
| 3 | | |
| 4 | | |
| 5 | | |
| 6 | | |
| 7 | | |
| 8 | | |
| 9 | | |
| 10 | | |
| 11 | | |
| 12 | | |
| 13 | | |
| 14 | | |
| 15 | | |
| 16 | | |
| **TOTAL THIS SIDE** ENTER THIS TOTAL ON REVERSE SIDE | | |

**ENDORSE HERE**

For deposit
Daniel Jones

**DO NOT WRITE, STAMP OR SIGN BELOW THIS LINE**
RESERVED FOR FINANCIAL INSTITUTION USE*

*FEDERAL RESERVE BOARD OF GOVERNORS REG. CC

Please List Each Check Separately

| CHECKS | DOLLARS | CENTS |
|--------|---------|-------|
| 1 | | |
| 2 | | |
| 3 | | |
| 4 | | |
| 5 | | |
| 6 | | |
| 7 | | |
| 8 | | |
| 9 | | |
| 10 | | |
| 11 | | |
| 12 | | |
| 13 | | |
| 14 | | |
| 15 | | |
| 16 | | |
| **TOTAL THIS SIDE** ENTER THIS TOTAL ON REVERSE SIDE | | |

Please List Each Check Separately

| CHECKS | DOLLARS | CENTS |
|--------|---------|-------|
| 1 | | |
| 2 | | |
| 3 | | |
| 4 | | |
| 5 | | |
| 6 | | |
| 7 | | |
| 8 | | |
| 9 | | |
| 10 | | |
| 11 | | |
| 12 | | |
| 13 | | |
| 14 | | |
| 15 | | |
| 16 | | |
| **TOTAL THIS SIDE** ENTER THIS TOTAL ON REVERSE SIDE | | |

**ENDORSE HERE**

For Deposit
Lella S. Petrosina

**DO NOT WRITE, STAMP OR SIGN BELOW THIS LINE**
RESERVED FOR FINANCIAL INSTITUTION USE*

*FEDERAL RESERVE BOARD OF GOVERNORS REG. CC

**ENDORSE HERE**

For Deposit
Lella Petrosina

**DO NOT WRITE, STAMP OR SIGN BELOW THIS LINE**
RESERVED FOR FINANCIAL INSTITUTION USE*

*FEDERAL RESERVE BOARD OF GOVERNORS REG. CC

HH299·171·482

May 18, 19--

Linda Scott

Ramsey Scott

---

HH299·171·483

May 18, 19--

Linda Scott

Ramsey Scott

---

HH299·171·484

May 18, 19--

Linda Scott

Ramsey Scott

---

**RAILWAY RETIREMENT FUND**
DALLAS, TX 75154

452312  VI-12

32-934/1110

May 20        19 --          $876.44

PAY TO THE
ORDER OF    Robert D. Ramsey

Eight hundred seventy-six and 44/100 ------------ DOLLARS

FOR CLASSROOM USE ONLY

**Dallas METROPLEX Bank**
Dallas, Texas

FOR Mo. Retirement, #88632        Jack R. Shiplet

⑈⑈00934⑆⑆⑆452⑆2⑆684935271⑈

---

VI-12

| C A S H | CURRENCY | | |
|---|---|---|---|
| | COIN | | |
| CHECKS (LIST SINGLY) | | | |
| 452312 | | 876 | 44 |
| TOTAL from reverse side | | | |
| **TOTAL** | | 876 | 44 |
| LESS CASH RECEIVED | | — | |
| **NET DEPOSIT** | | 876 | 44 |

**DEPOSIT TICKET**

USE OTHER SIDE FOR
ADDITIONAL LISTING

BE SURE EACH ITEM IS
PROPERLY ENDORSED

32-2/1110

FOR CLASSROOM USE ONLY

**ROBERT D. RAMSEY**
8424 ROCKBROOK ST.
DALLAS, TX 75134

DATE    5-18        19 --

SIGN HERE FOR LESS CASH RECEIVED

**Midtown Bank**
Dallas, Texas

⑆⑆⑆0000 20⑆     ⑈386493 2⑈

---

HH299·171·481

May 18, 19--

Linda Scott

Ramsey Scott

Please List Each Check Separately

| CHECKS | DOLLARS | CENTS |
|---|---|---|
| 1 | | |
| 2 | | |
| 3 | | |
| 4 | | |
| 5 | | |
| 6 | | |
| 7 | | |
| 8 | | |
| 9 | | |
| 10 | | |
| 11 | | |
| 12 | | |
| 13 | | |
| 14 | | |
| 15 | | |
| 16 | | |
| **TOTAL THIS SIDE** ENTER THIS TOTAL ON REVERSE SIDE | | |

For Deposit

Robert D. Ramsey

## SIMULATED CASH FOR DISBURSEMENT

**Currency:**

| | |
|---|---|
| Hundreds | $ |
| Fifties | $ |
| Twenties | $ |
| Tens | $ |
| Fives | $ |
| Ones | $ |

**Total Currency** $

**Coins:**

| | |
|---|---|
| Dollars | $ |
| Halves | $ |
| Quarters | $ |
| Dimes | $ |
| Nickels | $ |
| Pennies | $ |

**Total Coins**

**TOTAL CASH DISBURSED** $

(To Customer)

---

## SIMULATED CASH FOR DISBURSEMENT

**Currency:**

| | |
|---|---|
| Hundreds | $ |
| Fifties | $ |
| Twenties | $ |
| Tens | $ |
| Fives | $ |
| Ones | $ |

**Total Currency** $

**Coins:**

| | |
|---|---|
| Dollars | $ |
| Halves | $ |
| Quarters | $ |
| Dimes | $ |
| Nickels | $ |
| Pennies | $ |

**Total Coins**

**TOTAL CASH DISBURSED** $

(To Customer)

---

## SIMULATED CASH FOR DISBURSEMENT

**Currency:**

| | |
|---|---|
| Hundreds | $ |
| Fifties | $ |
| Twenties | $ |
| Tens | $ |
| Fives | $ |
| Ones | $ |

**Total Currency** $

**Coins:**

| | |
|---|---|
| Dollars | $ |
| Halves | $ |
| Quarters | $ |
| Dimes | $ |
| Nickels | $ |
| Pennies | $ |

**Total Coins**

**TOTAL CASH DISBURSED** $

(To Customer)

---

## SIMULATED CASH RECEIVED

**Currency:**

| | | |
|---|---|---|
| | Hundreds | $ |
| | Fifties | $ |
| 5 | Twenties | $ 100.00 |
| 5 | Tens | $ 50.00 |
| 7 | Fives | $ 35.00 |
| 25 | Ones | $ 25.00 |

**Total Currency** $ 210.00

**Coins:**

| | | |
|---|---|---|
| | Dollars | $ |
| | Halves | $ |
| 1 roll | Quarters | $ 10.00 |
| 1 roll | Dimes | $ 5.00 |
| 1 roll | Nickels | $ 2.00 |
| 2 rolls | Pennies | $ 1.00 |

**Total Coins** $ 18.00

**TOTAL CASH RECEIVED** $ 228.00

(To Teller Drawer)

---

## SIMULATED CASH FOR DISBURSEMENT

**Currency:**

| | |
|---|---|
| Hundreds | $ |
| Fifties | $ |
| Twenties | $ |
| Tens | $ |
| Fives | $ |
| Ones | $ |

**Total Currency** $

**Coins:**

| | |
|---|---|
| Dollars | $ |
| Halves | $ |
| Quarters | $ |
| Dimes | $ |
| Nickels | $ |
| Pennies | $ |

**Total Coins**

**TOTAL CASH DISBURSED** $

(To Customer)

---

## SIMULATED CASH FOR DISBURSEMENT

**Currency:**

| | |
|---|---|
| Hundreds | $ |
| Fifties | $ |
| Twenties | $ |
| Tens | $ |
| Fives | $ |
| Ones | $ |

**Total Currency** $

**Coins:**

| | |
|---|---|
| Dollars | $ |
| Halves | $ |
| Quarters | $ |
| Dimes | $ |
| Nickels | $ |
| Pennies | $ |

**Total Coins**

**TOTAL CASH DISBURSED** $

(To Customer)

# TRANSACTION REQUEST FORM

**Midtown Bank**
Dallas, Texas

**Name** _____  **Date** _____

**Account #** _____  **Teller** _____

## DEPOSIT   Acct. Type: Checking ☐ Savings ☐

| | | |
|---|---|---|
| **Cash** | | |
| **Checks** | | |
| | | |
| | | |
| | | |
| | | |
| **Total Received** | | |
| **Less Cash Received** | | |
| **Net Deposit** | | |

### WITHDRAWAL

Checking    $_____
Savings     $_____

### TRANSFER

$_____
From Acct. # _____
To Acct. # _____

**Signature** _____

---

# TRANSACTION REQUEST FORM

**Midtown Bank**
Dallas, Texas

**Name** _Amy Eddings_   **Date** _____

**Account #** _542-941-6_   **Teller** _____

## DEPOSIT   Acct. Type: Checking ☐ Savings ☐

| | | |
|---|---|---|
| **Cash** | | |
| **Checks** | | |
| | | |
| | | |
| | | |
| | | |
| **Total Received** | | |
| **Less Cash Received** | | |
| **Net Deposit** | | |

### WITHDRAWAL

Checking    $_____
Savings     $_____

### TRANSFER

$_____
From Acct. # _____
To Acct. # _____

**Signature** _____

---

# TRANSACTION REQUEST FORM

**Midtown Bank**
Dallas, Texas

**Name** _____  **Date** _____

**Account #** _____  **Teller** _____

## DEPOSIT   Acct. Type: Checking ☐ Savings ☐

| | | |
|---|---|---|
| **Cash** | | |
| **Checks** | | |
| | | |
| | | |
| | | |
| | | |
| **Total Received** | | |
| **Less Cash Received** | | |
| **Net Deposit** | | |

### WITHDRAWAL

Checking    $_____
Savings     $_____

### TRANSFER

$_____
From Acct. # _____
To Acct. # _____

**Signature** _____

## VI-15 — Deposit Ticket

**EDWARD L. EATON**
5109 DIXON STREET
DALLAS, TX 75181

DATE May 18 19 —

**Midtown Bank**
Dallas, Texas

SIGN HERE FOR LESS CASH RECEIVED

⑈⑈10000 20⑈ "386904 2⑈"

**DEPOSIT TICKET**

USE OTHER SIDE FOR
ADDITIONAL LISTING

BE SURE EACH ITEM IS
PROPERLY ENDORSED

| | CURRENCY | 210 | — |
|---|---|---|---|
| C A S H | COIN | 18 | — |
| CHECKS (LIST SINGLY) | Aston Dynamic | 697 521 | 43 68 |
| | | | |
| | TOTAL from reverse side | | |
| | **TOTAL** | 1,447 | 11 |
| | LESS CASH RECEIVED | | |
| | **NET DEPOSIT** | 1,447 | 11 |

FOR CLASSROOM USE ONLY

---

## VI-16 — Check 0765

0765

32-2/1110

**WING S. KUO**
72036 OVERDOWNS DRIVE
DALLAS, TX 75240

May 18 19 —

PAY TO THE ORDER OF  Mark Phillips   $30.00

Thirty and no/100 ——————— DOLLARS

**Midtown Bank**
Dallas, Texas

FOR Yardwork

Wing S. Kuo

⑈⑈10000 20⑈0765 6839456⑈"

FOR CLASSROOM USE ONLY

---

## VI-18 — Check 11542

11542

32-11/1110

**ECLECTIC HOMES**
3524 GREENVIEW DRIVE
DALLAS, TX 75050

5/14 19 —

PAY TO THE ORDER OF  Dale F. Sharp   $2,564.98

two thousand five hundred sixty-four and 98/100 DOLLARS

NORTHSIDE FEDERAL BANK      DALLAS TEXAS

FOR

Honor Sims

⑈⑈10000 326⑈⑈1542 37565523⑈"

FOR CLASSROOM USE ONLY

---

## VI-14 — Check 3211

3211

32-2/1110

**BENJAMIN M. AND DOROTHY S. RICHARDSON**
9968 NANCY LANE
DALLAS, TX 75134

May 18 19 —

PAY TO THE ORDER OF  Cash   $150.00

One hundred and no/100 ——————— DOLLARS

**Midtown Bank**
Dallas, Texas

FOR

Benjamin M. Richardson

⑈⑈10000 20⑈321⑈ 3615974⑈"

FOR CLASSROOM USE ONLY

---

## VI-15 — Check 8661

8661

192-41/1119

**Aston & McCall**
67432 Kentwood Lane
Carrollton, Texas 75056

5-15 19 —

PAY TO THE ORDER OF  Edward Eaton   $697.43

Six hundred ninety-seven and 43/100 ——— DOLLARS

**Addison Bank**
Addison, Texas

MEMO

Jerry Adler

⑈⑈1900⑈⑈8661⑈ 768 2455⑈"

FOR CLASSROOM USE ONLY

---

## VI-15 — Check 7663

7663

32-3958/1110

**DYNAMIC INSULATION CO.**
5421 PRESIDIO AVE.
DALLAS, TX 75216

May 16 19 —

PAY TO THE ORDER OF  Ed Eaton   $521.68

Five hundred twenty-one and 68/100 DOLLARS

**Fair Park Bank**
Dallas, Texas

FOR

Gabriel Arbelo

⑈⑈103958⑈7663⑈ 73690 23⑈"

FOR CLASSROOM USE ONLY

**ENDORSE HERE**

_____

_____

_____

**DO NOT WRITE, STAMP OR SIGN BELOW THIS LINE**
RESERVED FOR FINANCIAL INSTITUTION USE*

*FEDERAL RESERVE BOARD OF GOVERNORS REG. CC

**ENDORSE HERE**

_For Deposit_
_Edward Eaton_

_____

_____

**DO NOT WRITE, STAMP OR SIGN BELOW THIS LINE**
RESERVED FOR FINANCIAL INSTITUTION USE*

*FEDERAL RESERVE BOARD OF GOVERNORS REG. CC

**ENDORSE HERE**

_For Deposit_
_Ed Eaton_

_____

_____

**DO NOT WRITE, STAMP OR SIGN BELOW THIS LINE**
RESERVED FOR FINANCIAL INSTITUTION USE*

*FEDERAL RESERVE BOARD OF GOVERNORS REG. CC

Please List Each Check Separately

| CHECKS | DOLLARS | CENTS |
|--------|---------|-------|
| 1 | | |
| 2 | | |
| 3 | | |
| 4 | | |
| 5 | | |
| 6 | | |
| 7 | | |
| 8 | | |
| 9 | | |
| 10 | | |
| 11 | | |
| 12 | | |
| 13 | | |
| 14 | | |
| 15 | | |
| 16 | | |
| **TOTAL THIS SIDE** ENTER THIS TOTAL ON REVERSE SIDE | | |

**ENDORSE HERE**

_____

_____

_____

**DO NOT WRITE, STAMP OR SIGN BELOW THIS LINE**
RESERVED FOR FINANCIAL INSTITUTION USE*

*FEDERAL RESERVE BOARD OF GOVERNORS REG. CC

**ENDORSE HERE**

_For deposit_
_Dale F. Sharp_
_#4837925_

**DO NOT WRITE, STAMP OR SIGN BELOW THIS LINE**
RESERVED FOR FINANCIAL INSTITUTION USE*

*FEDERAL RESERVE BOARD OF GOVERNORS REG. CC

## TRANSACTION REQUEST FORM

**Midtown Bank**
Dallas, Texas

**Name** Mauricio Alvarez

**Account #** 396-501-2

**Date**

**Teller**

**DEPOSIT**   Acct. Type: Checking ☐   Savings ☐

| | |
|---|---|
| Cash | |
| Checks | |
| | |
| | |
| | |
| | |
| | |
| Total Received | |
| Less Cash Received | |
| Net Deposit | |

**WITHDRAWAL**

Checking   $_____

Savings   $_____

**TRANSFER**

$_____

From Acct. # _____

To Acct. # _____

Signature

---

## TRANSACTION REQUEST FORM

**Midtown Bank**
Dallas, Texas

**Name** Thomas Jones

**Account #**

**Date**

**Teller**

**DEPOSIT**   Acct. Type: Checking ☐   Savings ☐

| | |
|---|---|
| Cash | |
| Checks | |
| | |
| | |
| | |
| | |
| | |
| Total Received | |
| Less Cash Received | |
| Net Deposit | |

**WITHDRAWAL**

Checking   $_____

Savings   $_____

**TRANSFER**

$_____

From Acct. # 591-684-2

To Acct. # 591-684-3

Signature

---

**SIMULATED CASH RECEIVED**

Currency:

| | | |
|---|---|---|
| Hundreds | $ | 100.00 |
| Fifties | $ | |
| Twenties | $ | |
| Tens | $ | |
| Fives | $ | |
| Ones | $ | 50.00 |
| **Total Currency** | $ | 150.00 |

Coins:

| | | |
|---|---|---|
| Dollars | $ | |
| Halves | $ | 10.00 |
| Quarters | $ | 50.00 |
| Dimes | $ | 40.00 |
| Nickels | $ | 28.00 |
| Pennies | $ | 14.00 |
| **Total Coins** | $ | 142.00 |
| **TOTAL CASH RECEIVED** | $ | 292.00 |

(To Teller Drawer)

Currency: 1 / 50

Coins: 1 roll / 5 rolls / 8 rolls / 12 rolls / 28 rolls

---

**SIMULATED CASH FOR DISBURSEMENT**

Currency:

| | | |
|---|---|---|
| Hundreds | $ | |
| Fifties | $ | |
| Twenties | $ | |
| Tens | $ | |
| Fives | $ | |
| Ones | $ | |
| **Total Currency** | | |

Coins:

| | | |
|---|---|---|
| Dollars | $ | |
| Halves | $ | |
| Quarters | $ | |
| Dimes | $ | |
| Nickels | $ | |
| Pennies | $ | |
| **Total Coins** | | |
| **TOTAL CASH DISBURSED** | $ | |

(To Customer)

## Check 38574 (VI-22)

**EXCEL OFFICE PRODUCTS**
56432 MAY STREET
DALLAS, TX 75208

38574

32-801/1110

May 6 19 --

PAY TO THE ORDER OF ___ Flack Electronics ___ $3,561.14

Three thousand five hundred sixty-one and 14/100 DOLLARS

**DOWNTOWN BANK** DALLAS, TEXAS

FOR CLASSROOM USE ONLY

FOR inv. 69466

Esther Bond

⑈1⑈008015⑈38574⑈ 13467894⑈

---

## Check 0786 (VI-22)

**CHARLOTTE S. KEESEE**
5432 MARSH LANE
DALLAS, TX 75050

0786

60-14/1119

May 9 19 --

PAY TO THE ORDER OF ___ Flack Electronics ___ $102.54

One hundred two and 54/100 ___ DOLLARS

**SECURITY STATE BANK**
CARROLLTON, TEXAS

FOR CLASSROOM USE ONLY

FOR charges

Charlotte S. Keesee

⑈119004440786⑈ 475638 29⑈

---

## Check 8722 (VI-22)

**ABCD OFFICE EQUIPMENT**
4321 LANGSTON
DALLAS, TX 75235

8722

32-9635/1110

5/11 19 --

PAY TO THE ORDER OF ___ Flack Electronics ___ $916.58

Nine Hundred Sixteen and 58/100 ___ DOLLARS

**LNB Local National Bank**
Dallas, Texas

FOR CLASSROOM USE ONLY

FOR inv. 69480

Allen Anthony

⑈11096353⑈8722⑈ 56473829⑈

---

## Deposit Ticket (VI-18)

**DALE F. OR MONICA L. SHARP**
1408 TURTLE CREEK BLVD.
DALLAS, TX 75219

32-2/1110

DATE May 18 19 --

**DEPOSIT TICKET**

USE OTHER SIDE FOR
ADDITIONAL LISTING

BE SURE EACH ITEM IS
PROPERLY ENDORSED

| | | CURRENCY | |
|---|---|---|---|
| C A S H | | COIN | |
| CHECKS (LIST SINGLY) | | | |
| | Sims | 2,504 | 98 |
| TOTAL from reverse side | | | |
| TOTAL | | | |
| LESS CASH RECEIVED | | | |
| **NET DEPOSIT** | | 2,504 | 98 |

FOR CLASSROOM USE ONLY

**Midtown Bank**
Dallas, Texas

SIGN HERE FOR LESS CASH RECEIVED

⑈1100002001⑈ 483792511⑈

---

## Check 8766 (VI-21)

**Harold's Pet Boutique**
123 Town East Blvd.
Dallas, Texas 75016

8766

67-305/1119

May 17 19 --

PAY TO THE ORDER OF ___ Kenneth R. Titus ___ $581.70

Five hundred eighty-one and 70/100 ___ DOLLARS

**Garland State Bank**
GARLAND, TEXAS

FOR CLASSROOM USE ONLY

FOR payroll

Harold Owens

⑈119030571⑈8766⑈ 5753829⑈

---

## Deposit Ticket (VI-22)

**FLACK ELECTRONICS**
5719 LIVE OAK AVENUE
DALLAS, TX 75206

32-2/1110

DATE May 18 19 --

**DEPOSIT TICKET**

USE OTHER SIDE FOR
ADDITIONAL LISTING

BE SURE EACH ITEM IS
PROPERLY ENDORSED

| | | CURRENCY | |
|---|---|---|---|
| C A S H | | COIN | |
| CHECKS (LIST SINGLY) | | | |
| | 34561 | 453 | 29 |
| | 8722 | 966 | 58 |
| TOTAL from reverse side | | 3,663 | 68 |
| TOTAL | | 5,083 | 55 |
| LESS CASH RECEIVED | | | |
| **NET DEPOSIT** | | 5,083 | 55 |

FOR CLASSROOM USE ONLY

**Midtown Bank**
Dallas, Texas

SIGN HERE FOR LESS CASH RECEIVED

⑈1100002001⑈ 645386 21⑈

| CHECKS | DOLLARS | CENTS |
|---|---|---|
| 1 | | |
| 2 | | |
| 3 | | |
| 4 | | |
| 5 | | |
| 6 | | |
| 7 | | |
| 8 | | |
| 9 | | |
| 10 | | |
| 11 | | |
| 12 | | |
| 13 | | |
| 14 | | |
| 15 | | |
| 16 | | |
| **TOTAL THIS SIDE** ENTER THIS TOTAL ON REVERSE SIDE | | |

**ENDORSE HERE**

*Kenneth R. Titus*

**DO NOT WRITE, STAMP OR SIGN BELOW THIS LINE**
RESERVED FOR FINANCIAL INSTITUTION USE*

*FEDERAL RESERVE BOARD OF GOVERNORS REG. CC

| CHECKS | DOLLARS | CENTS |
|---|---|---|
| 1 | 786 | 102 | 54 |
| 2 | 38574 | 3,561 | 14 |
| 3 | | |
| 4 | | |
| 5 | | |
| 6 | | |
| 7 | | |
| 8 | | |
| 9 | | |
| 10 | | |
| 11 | | |
| 12 | | |
| 13 | | |
| 14 | | |
| 15 | | |
| 16 | | |
| **TOTAL THIS SIDE** ENTER THIS TOTAL ON REVERSE SIDE | 3,663 | 68 |

**ENDORSE HERE**

*Flack Electronics
for deposit*

**DO NOT WRITE, STAMP OR SIGN BELOW THIS LINE**
RESERVED FOR FINANCIAL INSTITUTION USE*

*FEDERAL RESERVE BOARD OF GOVERNORS REG. CC

**ENDORSE HERE**

*Flack Electronics
for deposit*

**DO NOT WRITE, STAMP OR SIGN BELOW THIS LINE**
RESERVED FOR FINANCIAL INSTITUTION USE*

*FEDERAL RESERVE BOARD OF GOVERNORS REG. CC

**ENDORSE HERE**

*Flack Electronics
for deposit*

**DO NOT WRITE, STAMP OR SIGN BELOW THIS LINE**
RESERVED FOR FINANCIAL INSTITUTION USE*

*FEDERAL RESERVE BOARD OF GOVERNORS REG. CC

**MR. OR MRS. ALFRED C. DARROW**
9433 BASELINE DR.
DALLAS, TX 75243

1218

32-2/1110

May 18 19 —

PAY TO THE
ORDER OF _Midtown Bank_ $ 16.00

_Sixteen and no/100_ — — — DOLLARS

Midtown Bank
Dallas, Texas

FOR _____ Mrs. Alfred C. Darrow

FOR CLASSROOM USE ONLY

⑆11⑆0000 20⑆ 1218 ⑈864349⑈

---

DEPOSIT TICKET

USE OTHER SIDE FOR
ADDITIONAL LISTING

32-2/1110

| | | CURRENCY | | |
|---|---|---|---|---|
| C A S H | | COIN | | |
| CHECKS (LIST SINGLY) | | | | |
| | Drevor | 2,156 | 78 | |
| | | | | |
| | | | | |
| | TOTAL from reverse side | | | |
| | **TOTAL** | 2,156 | 78 | |
| | LESS CASH RECEIVED | | | |
| | **NET DEPOSIT** | 2,156 | 78 | |

BE SURE EACH ITEM IS
PROPERLY ENDORSED

FOR CLASSROOM USE ONLY

SIGN HERE FOR LESS CASH RECEIVED

May 18 19 —

Midtown Bank
Dallas, Texas

DATE _____

⑆11⑆0000 20⑆ ⑈69108 65⑈

---

DREVER DRILLING CO.
5643 S. Avenue W
Dallas, TX 75208

78622

32-150/1110

May 16 19 — —

PAY TO THE
ORDER OF _Janis B. Wall_ $ 2,156.78

Two thousand one hundred fifty-six and 78/100————————— DOLLARS

Federal Dallas Bank
Dallas, Texas

FOR _Payroll_

FOR CLASSROOM USE ONLY

Oliver Drever

⑆11001500⑆ 7862 ⑈574 62389⑈

---

**JANIS B. WALL**
7215 RIDGECREST DR.
DALLAS, TX 75231

---

**JARED L. SMITSON, ELECTRICAL CONT.**
52180 MERIMAC
DALLAS, TEXAS 75206

34561

32-29/1110

May 15 19 —

PAY TO THE
ORDER OF _Flack Electric_ $ 453.29

_Four hundred fifty-three and 29/100_ DOLLARS

CNB COMMUNITY
NATIONAL BANK
Dallas, Texas

FOR _Inv. 694856_ Jared L. Smitson

FOR CLASSROOM USE ONLY

⑆11⑆0000 29⑆ 34561 ⑈5813 24356⑈

---

**HUANG AND HUANG**
7946 WALNUT HILL
DALLAS, TX 75230

3410

32-2/1110

May 18 19 — —

PAY TO THE
ORDER OF _Cash_ $ 100.00

_One hundred and 00/100_ — — — DOLLARS

Midtown Bank
Dallas, Texas

FOR _____ Meiling Huang

FOR CLASSROOM USE ONLY

⑆11⑆0000 20⑆ 3410 ⑈4 9368 25⑈

---

## REQUEST FOR CUSTOMER INFORMATION

**Name** _____

**Acct. No.** _____

**Acct. Type** _____

**Last Deposit** _____

**Comments** _____

Please List Each Check Separately

| CHECKS | DOLLARS | CENTS |
|---|---|---|
| 1 | | |
| 2 | | |
| 3 | | |
| 4 | | |
| 5 | | |
| 6 | | |
| 7 | | |
| 8 | | |
| 9 | | |
| 10 | | |
| 11 | | |
| 12 | | |
| 13 | | |
| 14 | | |
| 15 | | |
| 16 | | |
| **TOTAL THIS SIDE** ENTER THIS TOTAL ON REVERSE SIDE | | |

**1112** (VI-29)

32-1076/1110

MR. OR MRS. BUFORD BURWOOD
4532 BARCLAY ST.
DALLAS, TX 75227

May 12 19 —

PAY TO THE
ORDER OF _Gordon Eye Associates_ $ 92.00

_Ninety-two and no/100_ ———————— DOLLARS

**S**ECURITY FIRST BANK
DALLAS, TEXAS

FOR _____

Buford Burwood

⑆111010768⑆1112⑆8768763 4⑈

---

**5643** (VI-29)

32-11/1110

KOLASCZ OPTICALS
5667 BOWSER
DALLAS, TX 75219

May 15 19 —

PAY TO THE
ORDER OF _Gordon Eye Associates_ $ 196.48

_One hundred ninety-six and 48/100_ ———— DOLLARS

**N**ORTHSIDE
**F**EDERAL
**B**ANK
DALLAS
TEXAS

FOR _Supplies_

O.R. Kolascz

⑆110003 26⑆5643⑆55433 2 1⑈

---

**1478** (VI-29)

32-69/1110

JOSEPH P. OR CHRISTINE PETERSON
4637 NEW ORLEANS PLACE
DALLAS, TX 75202

5-16 19 —

PAY TO THE
ORDER OF _Gordon Eye Associates_ $ 65.00

_Sixty-five and no/100_ ———————— DOLLARS

**S**outhside Bank
Dallas, Texas

FOR _____

Joseph P. Peterson

⑆110006 91⑆1478⑆1445738 9⑈

---

(VI-29)

32-2/1110

**DEPOSIT TICKET**

USE OTHER SIDE FOR
ADDITIONAL LISTING

BE SURE EACH ITEM IS
PROPERLY ENDORSED

| C | CURRENCY | | |
| A | COIN | | |
| S H | | | |
| CHECKS (LIST SINGLY) | | | |
| Cavett | | 50 | — |
| Burwood | | 92 | — |
| TOTAL from reverse side | | 393 | 98 |
| **TOTAL** | | 535 | 98 |
| LESS CASH RECEIVED | | | |
| **NET DEPOSIT** | | 535 | 98 |

FOR CLASSROOM USE ONLY

GORDON EYE ASSOCIATES
DALLAS, TX 75230

DATE _May 18_ 19 —

SIGN HERE FOR LESS CASH RECEIVED

**Midtown Bank**
Dallas, Texas

⑆110000 20⑈ ⑆891697 3⑈

---

**2115** (VI-29)

32-3958/1110

ELVA OR ROYCE T. INMAN
48576 MILL RUN ROAD
DALLAS, TX 75206

May 11 19 —

PAY TO THE
ORDER OF _Gordon Eye Associates_ $ 45.00

_Forty-five and no/100_ ——————— DOLLARS

**Fair Park Bank**
Dallas, Texas

FOR _eye exam_

Elva Inman

⑆110395 86⑆2115⑆574810 29 3⑈

---

**0786** (VI-29)

32-934/1110

RENE CAVETT
54432 SHADYBROOK LANE
DALLAS, TX 75206

May 14 19 —

PAY TO THE
ORDER OF _Gordon Eye Associates_ $ 50.00

_Fifty and no/100_ ——————————— DOLLARS

**Dallas METROPLEX Bank**
Dallas, Texas

FOR _____

Rene Cavett

⑆110093 45⑆0786⑆574463 29 8⑈

Please List Each Check Separately

| CHECKS | | DOLLARS | CENTS |
|---|---|---|---|
| 1 Inman | | 45 | — |
| 2 Peterson | | 65 | — |
| 3 Kolascz | | 196 | 48 |
| 4 Villaneuba | | 87 | 50 |
| 5 | | | |
| 6 | | | |
| 7 | | | |
| 8 | | | |
| 9 | | | |
| 10 | | | |
| 11 | | | |
| 12 | | | |
| 13 | | | |
| 14 | | | |
| 15 | | | |
| 16 | | | |
| **TOTAL THIS SIDE** ENTER THIS TOTAL ON REVERSE SIDE | | 393 | 98 |

**ENDORSE HERE**

Gordon Eye Associates

DO NOT WRITE, STAMP OR SIGN BELOW THIS LINE
RESERVED FOR FINANCIAL INSTITUTION USE*

*FEDERAL RESERVE BOARD OF GOVERNORS REG. CC

**ENDORSE HERE**

Gordon Eye Associates

DO NOT WRITE, STAMP OR SIGN BELOW THIS LINE
RESERVED FOR FINANCIAL INSTITUTION USE*

*FEDERAL RESERVE BOARD OF GOVERNORS REG. CC

**ENDORSE HERE**

Gordon Eye Associates

DO NOT WRITE, STAMP OR SIGN BELOW THIS LINE
RESERVED FOR FINANCIAL INSTITUTION USE*

*FEDERAL RESERVE BOARD OF GOVERNORS REG. CC

**ENDORSE HERE**

Gordon Eye Associates

DO NOT WRITE, STAMP OR SIGN BELOW THIS LINE
RESERVED FOR FINANCIAL INSTITUTION USE*

*FEDERAL RESERVE BOARD OF GOVERNORS REG. CC

**ENDORSE HERE**

Gordon Eye Associates

DO NOT WRITE, STAMP OR SIGN BELOW THIS LINE
RESERVED FOR FINANCIAL INSTITUTION USE*

*FEDERAL RESERVE BOARD OF GOVERNORS REG. CC

## SIMULATED CASH RECEIVED

**Currency:**

|  | Count |  | Amount |
|---|---|---|---|
| Hundreds |  | $ |  |
| Fifties |  | $ |  |
| Twenties | 10 | $ | 200.00 |
| Tens | 19 | $ | 190.00 |
| Fives | 27 | $ | 135.00 |
| Ones | 109 | $ | 109.00 |

**Total Currency** $ 634.00

**Coins:**

|  | Count |  | Amount |
|---|---|---|---|
| Dollars |  | $ |  |
| Halves |  | $ |  |
| Quarters | 87 | $ | 21.75 |
| Dimes | 21 | $ | 2.10 |
| Nickels | 15 | $ | .75 |
| Pennies | 11 | $ | .11 |

**Total Coins** $ 24.71

**TOTAL CASH RECEIVED** $ 658.71

(To Teller Drawer)

---

## SIMULATED CASH FOR DISBURSEMENT

**Currency:**

| Hundreds | $ |
|---|---|
| Fifties | $ |
| Twenties | $ |
| Tens | $ |
| Fives | $ |
| Ones | $ |

**Total Currency** $

**Coins:**

| Dollars | $ |
|---|---|
| Halves | $ |
| Quarters | $ |
| Dimes | $ |
| Nickels | $ |
| Pennies | $ |

**Total Coins** $

**TOTAL CASH DISBURSED** $

(To Customer)

---

## SIMULATED CASH FOR DISBURSEMENT

**Currency:**

| Hundreds | $ |
|---|---|
| Fifties | $ |
| Twenties | $ |
| Tens | $ |
| Fives | $ |
| Ones | $ |

**Total Currency** $

**Coins:**

| Dollars | $ |
|---|---|
| Halves | $ |
| Quarters | $ |
| Dimes | $ |
| Nickels | $ |
| Pennies | $ |

**Total Coins** $

**TOTAL CASH DISBURSED** $

(To Customer)

---

## SIMULATED CASH FOR DISBURSEMENT

**Currency:**

| Hundreds | $ |
|---|---|
| Fifties | $ |
| Twenties | $ |
| Tens | $ |
| Fives | $ |
| Ones | $ |

**Total Currency** $

**Coins:**

| Dollars | $ |
|---|---|
| Halves | $ |
| Quarters | $ |
| Dimes | $ |
| Nickels | $ |
| Pennies | $ |

**Total Coins** $

**TOTAL CASH DISBURSED** $

(To Customer)

---

## SIMULATED CASH RECEIVED

**Currency:**

|  | Count |  | Amount |
|---|---|---|---|
| Hundreds | 1 | $ | 100.00 |
| Fifties |  | $ |  |
| Twenties | 11 | $ | 220.00 |
| Tens | 14 | $ | 140.00 |
| Fives | 21 | $ | 105.00 |
| Ones | 57 | $ | 57.00 |

**Total Currency** $ 622.00

**Coins:**

| Dollars | $ |
|---|---|
| Halves | $ |
| Quarters | $ |
| Dimes | $ |
| Nickels | $ |
| Pennies | $ |

**Total Coins** $

**TOTAL CASH RECEIVED** $ 622.00

(To Teller Drawer)

---

## SIMULATED CASH FOR DISBURSEMENT

**Currency:**

| Hundreds | $ |
|---|---|
| Fifties | $ |
| Twenties | $ |
| Tens | $ |
| Fives | $ |
| Ones | $ |

**Total Currency** $

**Coins:**

| Dollars | $ |
|---|---|
| Halves | $ |
| Quarters | $ |
| Dimes | $ |
| Nickels | $ |
| Pennies | $ |

**Total Coins** $

**TOTAL CASH DISBURSED** $

(To Customer)

**Check 1453 — VI-31**

C. SCOTT JUDAY
67541 Custer Parkway
RICHARDSON, TEXAS 75080

32-76/1110

Date: May 14 19 —

PAY TO THE ORDER OF Underhill Animal Clinic    $28.51

Twenty-eight and 51/100 ——————— DOLLARS

*Northside State Bank*
*Dallas, Texas*

FOR _____    C. Scott Juday

FOR CLASSROOM USE ONLY

⑆⑈1000768⑈ 1453 ⑉756375841⑈

---

**Deposit Ticket — VI-31**

UNDERHILL ANIMAL CLINIC
514 SYCAMORE DRIVE
DALLAS, TX 75148

32-2/1110

DEPOSIT TICKET
USE OTHER SIDE FOR
ADDITIONAL LISTING

BE SURE EACH ITEM IS
PROPERLY ENDORSED

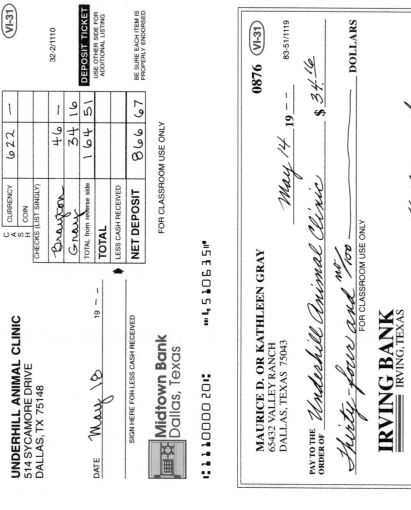

| C A S H | CURRENCY | 622 | — |
| | COIN | | — |
| CHECKS (LIST SINGLY) | | | |
| Brayton | | 46 | — |
| Gray | | 34 | 16 |
| TOTAL from reverse side | | 164 | 51 |
| **TOTAL** | | 866 | 67 |
| LESS CASH RECEIVED | | | |
| **NET DEPOSIT** | | 866 | 67 |

FOR CLASSROOM USE ONLY

DATE May 18 19 —

SIGN HERE FOR LESS CASH RECEIVED

**Midtown Bank**
Dallas, Texas

⑆110000 20⑈    ⑉45 10635⑈

---

**Check 0876 — VI-31**

MAURICE D. OR KATHLEEN GRAY
65432 VALLEY RANCH
DALLAS, TEXAS 75043

83-51/1119

May 14 19 —

PAY TO THE ORDER OF Underhill Animal Clinic    $34.16

Thirty-four and no/100 ——————— DOLLARS

**IRVING BANK**
IRVING, TEXAS

FOR _____    Kathleen Gray

FOR CLASSROOM USE ONLY

⑆1190050⑈0876⑈ 34 256892⑈

---

**Check 0612 — VI-29**

Maria T. or Jose R. Villaneuva
57364 Firelight Lane
Dallas, Texas 75248

192-41/1119

May 15 19 —

PAY TO THE ORDER OF Andron Eye Associates    $87.50

Eighty-seven and 50/100 ——————— DOLLARS

**Addison Bank**
Addison, Texas

MEMO _____    Maria T. Villaneuva

FOR CLASSROOM USE ONLY

⑆1190048⑈0612⑈ 574867581⑈

---

**Check 3462 — VI-30**

TINA L. INGRAM-RAMEY, C.P.A.
2958 MCCALLUM, SUITE 403
DALLAS, TX 75252

32-2/1110

May 18 19 —

PAY TO THE ORDER OF Midtown Bank    $200.00

Two hundred and no/100 ——————— DOLLARS

**Midtown Bank**
Dallas, Texas

FOR Cash    Tina L. Ingram-Ramey

FOR CLASSROOM USE ONLY

⑆110000 20⑈ 3462⑈684938 1⑈

---

**Check 0866 — VI-31**

HANNAH B. DORSEY
3758 OLD TROUP HIGHWAY
TYLER, TEXAS 75770

59-4702/1119

May 5 19 —

PAY TO THE ORDER OF Underhill Animal Clinic    $35.00

Thirty-five and no/100 ——————— DOLLARS

**National Tyler Bank**
TYLER, TEXAS

MEMO _____    Hannah B. Dorsey

FOR CLASSROOM USE ONLY

⑆1194702⑈0866⑈ 657224⑈

**ENDORSE HERE**

Underhill Animal Clinic
Acct. 451063S

DO NOT WRITE, STAMP OR SIGN BELOW THIS LINE
RESERVED FOR FINANCIAL INSTITUTION USE.

"FEDERAL RESERVE BOARD OF GOVERNORS REG. CC

---

**ENDORSE HERE**

Underhill Animal Clinic
Acct. 451063S

DO NOT WRITE, STAMP OR SIGN BELOW THIS LINE
RESERVED FOR FINANCIAL INSTITUTION USE.

"FEDERAL RESERVE BOARD OF GOVERNORS REG. CC

---

Please List Each Check Separately

| CHECKS | DOLLARS | CENTS |
|---|---|---|
| 1  McDonnell | 34 | — |
| 2  Cheddar | 42 | — |
| 3  Fassbender | 25 | — |
| 4  Tilbury | 28 | 51 |
| 5  Donald | 35 | — |
| 6 | | |
| 7 | | |
| 8 | | |
| 9 | | |
| 10 | | |
| 11 | | |
| 12 | | |
| 13 | | |
| 14 | | |
| 15 | | |
| 16 | | |
| TOTAL THIS SIDE
ENTER THIS TOTAL
ON REVERSE SIDE | 164 | 51 |

"FEDERAL RESERVE BOARD OF GOVERNORS REG. CC

DO NOT WRITE, STAMP OR SIGN BELOW THIS LINE
RESERVED FOR FINANCIAL INSTITUTION USE.

---

**ENDORSE HERE**

Rhoda Eye Associates

DO NOT WRITE, STAMP OR SIGN BELOW THIS LINE
RESERVED FOR FINANCIAL INSTITUTION USE.

"FEDERAL RESERVE BOARD OF GOVERNORS REG. CC

---

**ENDORSE HERE**

DO NOT WRITE, STAMP OR SIGN BELOW THIS LINE
RESERVED FOR FINANCIAL INSTITUTION USE.

"FEDERAL RESERVE BOARD OF GOVERNORS REG. CC

---

**ENDORSE HERE**

DO NOT WRITE, STAMP OR SIGN BELOW THIS LINE
RESERVED FOR FINANCIAL INSTITUTION USE.

"FEDERAL RESERVE BOARD OF GOVERNORS REG. CC

**2145** VI-31

PAM OR BRUCE BRAYTON
53526 BRUNSWICK DRIVE
DALLAS, TEXAS 75220

32-866/1110

May 16 19 —

PAY TO THE
ORDER OF _Underhill Animal Clinic_ $ 46.00

Forty-six and no/100 ———————— DOLLARS

_DALLAS COUNTY_
_CREDIT UNION_   Dallas, Texas

FOR _____

Bruce Brayton

⑆1100866⑆ 2145 ⑆ 564738 219⑈

FOR CLASSROOM USE ONLY

---

VI-32

DEPOSIT TICKET

USE OTHER SIDE FOR
ADDITIONAL LISTING

BE SURE EACH ITEM IS
PROPERLY ENDORSED

32-2/1110

| | C A S H | CURRENCY | | |
|---|---|---|---|---|
| | | COIN | | |
| | CHECKS (LIST SINGLY) | | | |
| | Bouvier | 659 | 43 | |
| | TOTAL from reverse side | | | |
| | **TOTAL** | 659 | 43 | |
| | LESS CASH RECEIVED | | | |
| | **NET DEPOSIT** | 659 | 43 | |

FOR CLASSROOM USE ONLY

KELLY OR JACK C. MORGAN
2503 LARAMIE DRIVE
DALLAS, TX 75149

DATE _May 18_ 19 __

SIGN HERE FOR LESS CASH RECEIVED

**Midtown Bank**
Dallas, Texas

⑆110000020⑆    ⑈30645 2 2⑈

---

**1256** VI-32

JOHN AUSTIN BOUVIER
776 DAWSON COURT
DALLAS, TX 75081

48-38/1119

May 15 19 —

PAY TO THE
ORDER OF _Kelly Morgan_ $ 659.43

Six hundred fifty-nine and 43/100 ———— DOLLARS

_Second Bank of Plano_
PLANO, TEXAS

FOR _____

John Austin Bouvier

⑆1190038 5⑆ 1256 ⑆ 564768 7⑈

FOR CLASSROOM USE ONLY

---

**5631** VI-31

DEBRA OR CLINT MCDONNELL
2008 SAN JACINTO
DALLAS, TX 75202

32-69/1110

May 12 19 —

PAY TO THE
ORDER OF _Underhill Animal Clinic_ $ 34.00

Thirty-four and no/100 ———————— DOLLARS

**Southside Bank**
Dallas, Texas

FOR _____

Debra McDonnell

⑆1100069⑆ 5631 ⑆ 573625160⑈

FOR CLASSROOM USE ONLY

---

**0267** VI-31

LUIS OR MARTA PESCADOR
7110 SUNNY SLOPE DRIVE
DALLAS, TX 75206

32-3958/1110

May 13 19 —

PAY TO THE
ORDER OF _Underhill Animal Clinic_ $ 25.00

Twenty-five and no/100 ———————— DOLLARS

**Fair Park Bank**
Dallas, Texas

FOR _____

Luis Pescador

⑆1103958 6⑆ 0267 ⑆ 36 2759664⑈

FOR CLASSROOM USE ONLY

---

**2315** VI-31

Suellen or William G. Craddock
5632 Old Seagoeville Rd.
Dallas, Texas 75253

392-95/1119

May 15 19 —

PAY TO THE
ORDER OF _Underhill Animal Clinic_ $ 42.00

Forty-two and 00/100 ———————— DOLLARS

**Greater Mesquite Bank**
Mesquite • Texas

FOR _____

Suellen Craddock

⑆119000959⑆ 2315 ⑆ 46 1089 2⑈

FOR CLASSROOM USE ONLY

Please List Each Check Separately

| CHECKS | DOLLARS | CENTS |
|---|---|---|
| 1 | | |
| 2 | | |
| 3 | | |
| 4 | | |
| 5 | | |
| 6 | | |
| 7 | | |
| 8 | | |
| 9 | | |
| 10 | | |
| 11 | | |
| 12 | | |
| 13 | | |
| 14 | | |
| 15 | | |
| 16 | | |
| **TOTAL THIS SIDE** ENTER THIS TOTAL ON REVERSE SIDE | | |

# TRANSACTION REQUEST FORM

**Midtown Bank**
Dallas, Texas

**Name** F. D. Gibbs  **Date** _____

**Account #** _____  **Teller** _____

## DEPOSIT   Acct. Type: Checking ☐ Savings ☐

| | | |
|---|---|---|
| Cash | | |
| Checks | | |
| | | |
| | | |
| | | |
| | | |
| Total Received | | |
| Less Cash Received | | |
| Net Deposit | | |

## WITHDRAWAL

Checking   $_____
Savings   $_____

## TRANSFER

$_____
From Acct. # _____
To Acct. # 486-801-1

**Signature** _____

---

# TRANSACTION REQUEST FORM

**Midtown Bank**
Dallas, Texas

**Name** _____  **Date** _____

**Account #** _____  **Teller** _____

## DEPOSIT   Acct. Type: Checking ☐ Savings ☐

| | | |
|---|---|---|
| Cash | | |
| Checks | | |
| | | |
| | | |
| | | |
| | | |
| Total Received | | |
| Less Cash Received | | |
| Net Deposit | | |

## WITHDRAWAL

Checking   $_____
Savings   $_____

## TRANSFER

$_____
From Acct. # _____
To Acct. # _____

**Signature** _____

---

# TRANSACTION REQUEST FORM

**Midtown Bank**
Dallas, Texas

**Name** Shelly C. Wiemer  **Date** _____

**Account #** _____  **Teller** _____

## DEPOSIT   Acct. Type: Checking ☐ Savings ☐

| | | |
|---|---|---|
| Cash | | |
| Checks | | |
| | | |
| | | |
| | | |
| | | |
| Total Received | | |
| Less Cash Received | | |
| Net Deposit | | |

## WITHDRAWAL

Checking   $_____
Savings   $_____

## TRANSFER

$_____
From Acct. # _____
To Acct. # _____

**Signature** _____

## Check 1213

1213  VI-35
32-1076/1110

**CARRIE CLAYTON**
46372 KELLOGG
DALLAS, TX 75216

May 12   19 —

PAY TO THE ORDER OF _Jorgenson Arts and Collectibles_   $ 11.60

_Seventeen and 60/100_ ———————————— DOLLARS

**SECURITY FIRST BANK**
DALLAS, TEXAS

FOR _____

Carrie Clayton

⑈1110768⑈1213⑈574635 29⑈

---

## Check 0823

0823  VI-35
32-69/1110

**LEONA OR M. L. AUTRY**
543123 BOURQUIN
DALLAS, TX 75210

May 17   19 —

PAY TO THE ORDER OF _Jorgenson Arts and Collectibles_   $ 58.00

_fifty-eight and 00/100_ ———————————— DOLLARS

**Southside Bank**
Dallas, Texas

FOR _____

Leona Autry

⑈110069⑈0823⑈456689 263⑈

---

## Check 0459

0459  VI-35
83-1010/1119

**Julio or Consuelo Mota**
1354 Sundance
Irving, TX 75063

May 15   19 —

PAY TO THE ORDER OF _Jorgenson Arts & Collectibles_   $ 65.00

_Sixty-five and 00/100_ ———————————— DOLLARS

**$rving $avings**   Irving, Texas

MEMO _____

Consuelo Mota

⑈1110103⑈0459⑈354 6788⑈

---

## Check 1348

1348  VI-34
32-2/1110

**LINDA J. SCOTT, M.D.**
4017 SOUTHVIEW DR.
DALLAS, TX 75240

May 18   19 —

PAY TO THE ORDER OF _Midtown Bank_   $ 100.00

_One hundred and 00/100_ ———————————— DOLLARS

**Midtown Bank**
Dallas, Texas

FOR _Deposit #6943682_

Linda J. Scott

⑈1110000 20⑈1348⑈496384⑈

---

## Deposit Ticket

VI-35
32-2/1110

**JORGENSON ARTS AND COLLECTIBLES**
3411 UMPHRESS ROAD
DALLAS, TX 75217

DATE _May 18_   19 —

| | | DOLLARS | CENTS |
|---|---|---|---|
| CASH | CURRENCY | 634 | 00 |
| | COIN | 24 | 71 |
| CHECKS (LIST SINGLY) | | | |
| McBride | | 115 | 00 |
| Richardson | | 75 | 00 |
| TOTAL from reverse side | | 168 | 00 |
| **TOTAL** | | 1,016 | 71 |
| LESS CASH RECEIVED | | | |
| **NET DEPOSIT** | | 1,016 | 71 |

**DEPOSIT TICKET**

USE OTHER SIDE FOR ADDITIONAL LISTING

BE SURE EACH ITEM IS PROPERLY ENDORSED

SIGN HERE FOR LESS CASH RECEIVED

**Midtown Bank**
Dallas, Texas

⑈1110000 20⑈   ⑈58396 23⑈

---

## Check 1345

1345  VI-35
32-29/1110

**LORNA OR H. JULIAN STICKLES**
99123 SUNNYBROOK
DALLAS, TEXAS 75220

5-10   19 —

PAY TO THE ORDER OF _Jorgenson Arts & Collectibles_   $ 27.50

_Twenty-seven and 50/100_ ———————————— DOLLARS

**CNB COMMUNITY NATIONAL BANK**
Dallas, Texas

FOR _____

H. Julian Stickles

⑈1110000 29⑈1345⑈9093 1 256⑈

Please List Each Check Separately

| CHECKS | DOLLARS | CENTS |
|---|---|---|
| 1 Mota | 65 | 00 |
| 2 Autry | 58 | 00 |
| 3 Clayton | 17 | 60 |
| 4 Stickles | 27 | 50 |
| 5 | | |
| 6 | | |
| 7 | | |
| 8 | | |
| 9 | | |
| 10 | | |
| 11 | | |
| 12 | | |
| 13 | | |
| 14 | | |
| 15 | | |
| 16 | | |
| **TOTAL THIS SIDE** ENTER THIS TOTAL ON REVERSE SIDE | 168 | 00 |

Jorgenson

Arts and Collectibles

#5839623

Jorgenson

Arts and Collectibles

#5839623

Jorgenson

Arts and Collectibles

#5839623

Jorgenson

Arts and Collectibles

#5839623

# REQUEST FOR CUSTOMER INFORMATION (VI-38)

Name _____

Acct. No. _____

Acct. Type _____

Last Deposit _____

Comments _____

---

## (VI-35) 1568

MICHELLE OR MARVIN T. RICHARDSON
7743 MIDWAY ROAD
DALLAS, TX 75081

362-6/1119

May 16 19 —

PAY TO THE ORDER OF _Jorgenson Oston and Collection_ $ 75.00

_Seventy-five and no/100_ DOLLARS

**1 BANK AND TRUST**
RICHARDSON • TEXAS

FOR CLASSROOM USE ONLY

_Michelle Richardson_

FOR _____

⑆1190006⑈1568⑆36⑈8293⑈

---

## (VI-35) 1178

Alice or A. T. McBryde
16550 Audelia Road
Dallas, TX 75243

67-20/1119

May 15 19 —

Pay to the Order of _Jorgenson A. and C._ $ 115.00

_One hundred fifteen and no/100_ Dollars

**First Bank of Garland** Garland, Texas

FOR CLASSROOM USE ONLY

_A. T. McBryde_

Memo _____

⑆1190020⑈1178⑆46⑈33589⑈

---

## (VI-36) 9875

SAMMY'S SNACKS
1843 W. NW HIGHWAY
DALLAS, TX 75226

32-2/1110

19 —

PAY TO THE ORDER OF _____ $ _____

_____ DOLLARS

**Midtown Bank** Dallas, Texas

FOR CLASSROOM USE ONLY

FOR _____

⑆110000020⑈9875⑆33846⑈8⑈

---

## DEPOSIT TICKET (VI-39)

GOBLE AND DOUGLAS
1681 ARAPAHO ROAD
RICHARDSON, TEXAS 75080

32-2/1110

DATE May 18 19 —

| | | | |
|---|---|---|---|
| CASH | CURRENCY | | |
| | COIN | | |
| CHECKS (LIST SINGLY) | | | |
| _Ruvillu_ | | 176 | 00 |
| _Ames_ | | 324 | 58 |
| | | 1,310 | 00 |
| TOTAL from reverse side | | | |
| **TOTAL** | | | |
| LESS CASH RECEIVED | | | |
| **NET DEPOSIT** | | 1,810 | 58 |

USE OTHER SIDE FOR ADDITIONAL LISTING

BE SURE EACH ITEM IS PROPERLY ENDORSED

SIGN HERE FOR LESS CASH RECEIVED _____

**Midtown Bank** Dallas, Texas

FOR CLASSROOM USE ONLY

⑆1100020⑈ ⑆862543⑈

---

## (VI-39) 0257

Isenberger, Philip and Hilda
7654 Marsh Lane
Carrolton, Texas 75056

192-41/119

May 6 19 —

PAY TO THE ORDER OF _Noble and Douglas_ $ 275.00

_Two hundred seventy-five and no/100_ DOLLARS

**Addison Bank**
Addison, Texas

FOR CLASSROOM USE ONLY

_Philip Isenberger_
_Hilda Isenberger_

MEMO _____

⑆1190048⑈0257⑆5768245⑈

Please List Each Check Separately

| CHECKS | DOLLARS | CENTS |
|---|---|---|
| 1 Domke | 565 | 00 |
| 2 One Place | 745 | 00 |
| 3 | | |
| 4 | | |
| 5 | | |
| 6 | | |
| 7 | | |
| 8 | | |
| 9 | | |
| 10 | | |
| 11 | | |
| 12 | | |
| 13 | | |
| 14 | | |
| 15 | | |
| 16 | | |
| **TOTAL THIS SIDE** ENTER THIS TOTAL ON REVERSE SIDE | 1,310 | 00 |

**1555** (VI-39)

83-51/1119

BANISTER MOVIE RENTALS
35465 PARK SQUARE DRIVE
IRVING, TEXAS 75063

May 16 19——

PAY TO THE
ORDER OF _Stable and Douglas_ $176.00

_One hundred seventy-six and no/100_ ——————— DOLLARS

**IRVING BANK**
IRVING, TEXAS

FOR _____ _Adelaide Banister_

⑆ 11900510⑆ 1555 ⑆ 563 7 1 29 3 ⑈

---

(VI-40)

32-2/1110

USE OTHER SIDE FOR
ADDITIONAL LISTING

BE SURE EACH ITEM IS
PROPERLY ENDORSED

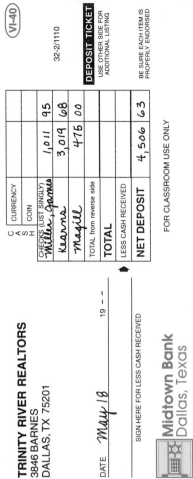

| | CURRENCY | | |
|---|---|---|---|
| C A S H | COIN | | |
| CHECKS (LIST SINGLY) _Miller, James_ | | 1,011 | 95 |
| _Kearns_ | | 3,019 | 68 |
| _Magill_ | | 475 | 00 |
| TOTAL from reverse side | | | |
| **TOTAL** | | | |
| LESS CASH RECEIVED | | | |
| **NET DEPOSIT** | | 4,506 | 63 |

FOR CLASSROOM USE ONLY

TRINITY RIVER REALTORS
3846 BARNES
DALLAS, TX 75201

DATE _May 18_ 19 — —

SIGN HERE FOR LESS CASH RECEIVED

**Midtown Bank**
Dallas, Texas

⑆ 1 10000 20 ⑆ ⑆ 456 38 15 ⑈

---

**2356** (VI-40)

32-534/1110

MILLER, JAMES & ROWE
ATTORNEYS AT LAW
DALLAS, TX 75142

May 12 19—— $1,011.95

_One thousand eleven and 95/100_ ——————— DOLLARS

**DALLAS BANK**
DALLAS, TEXAS

FOR _Arlington Property_ _Mildred James_

⑆ 110053 45 ⑆ 2356 ⑆ 387 16 2 7 ⑈

---

**3321** (VI-39)

32-934/1110

ONE PLACE APARTMENTS
46352 PRESTON ROAD
DALLAS, TX 75240

May 11 19—— $745.00

PAY TO THE
ORDER OF _Doble and Douglas_

_Seven hundred forty-five and 00/100_ ——————— DOLLARS

**Dallas METROPLEX Bank**
Dallas, Texas

FOR _____ _Antonia O'Toole_

⑆ 110093 45 ⑆ 33 2 1 ⑆ 5 7 48900 1 2 ⑈

---

**0341** (VI-39)

32-11/1110

KEVIN DOMKE
4535 ALTON ROAD
DALLAS, TX 75159

5-15 19—— $565.00

PAY TO THE
ORDER OF _Stable and Douglas_

_Five hundred sixty-five and no/100_ ——————— DOLLARS

**N**ORTHSIDE
**F**EDERAL     DALLAS
**B**ANK        TEXAS

FOR _____ _Kevin Domke_

⑆ 11000326 ⑆ 034 ⑆ 387 537 68 ⑈

---

**4432** (VI-39)

362-6/1119

KHALID OMERE
38574 OVERBROOK
DALLAS, TX 75248

May 15 19—— $324.58

PAY TO THE
ORDER OF _Stable and Douglas_

_Three hundred twenty-four and 58/100_ ~~~~~ DOLLARS

**1** BANK AND TRUST
RICHARDSON ● TEXAS

FOR _____ _Khalid Omere_

⑆ 11900069 ⑆ 44 3 ⑆ 463 758 3 ⑈

Please List Each Check Separately

| CHECKS | DOLLARS | CENTS |
|--------|---------|-------|
| 1 | | |
| 2 | | |
| 3 | | |
| 4 | | |
| 5 | | |
| 6 | | |
| 7 | | |
| 8 | | |
| 9 | | |
| 10 | | |
| 11 | | |
| 12 | | |
| 13 | | |
| 14 | | |
| 15 | | |
| 16 | | |
| TOTAL THIS SIDE ENTER THIS TOTAL ON REVERSE SIDE | | |

**KEARNS TITLE COMPANY**
6532 RIDGE ROAD
DALLAS, TEXAS 75201

78632  VI-40
32-29/1110

May 14  19 --

PAY TO THE ORDER OF _Trinity River Realtors_  $3,019.68

_Three thousand nineteen and_ 68/100 ———— DOLLARS

FOR CLASSROOM USE ONLY

**CNB** COMMUNITY
NATIONAL BANK
Dallas, Texas

_Belinda Kearns_

FOR _Bal. due_

⑈⑆1000 29⑆:⑆7863 2⑆⑆57 4635 29⑈

---

**TALMAGE REALTY OF DALLAS**
3837 STATLER
CARROLTON, TX 75056

7832  VI-41
32-11/1110

May 15  19 --

PAY TO THE ORDER OF _Dewey Scott_  $436.00

_Four hundred thirty-six and_ no/100 ———— DOLLARS

FOR CLASSROOM USE ONLY

**N**ORTHSIDE
**F**EDERAL
**B**ANK   DALLAS
TEXAS

_Otto Talmage_

FOR _Bal. rent_

⑈⑆1000 326⑆:⑆783 2⑆66 7390 265⑈

---

**Linda or Donald Magill**
76543 Pioneer Drive
Irving, TX 75063

4510  VI-40
83-1010/1119

May 15  19 --

PAY TO THE ORDER OF _Trinity River Realtors_  $475.00

_Four hundred seventy-five and_ no/100 DOLLARS

FOR CLASSROOM USE ONLY

**$**rving
**$**avings  Irving, Texas

_Linda Magill_

MEMO _Rent_

⑈⑆1191030⑆:4510⑆⑆76 30998 7⑈

---

**DEWEY E. SCOTT**
2168 NORTHWEST DR.
DALLAS, TX 75150

VI-41
32-2/1110

| | CURRENCY | | |
|---|---|---|---|
| C A S H | COIN | | |
| CHECKS (LIST SINGLY) | | | |
| | Cramer | 850 | 00 |
| | Talmage | 436 | 00 |
| | TOTAL from reverse side | | |
| **TOTAL** | | 1,286 | 00 |
| ← | LESS CASH RECEIVED | | |
| **NET DEPOSIT** | | 1,286 | 00 |

FOR CLASSROOM USE ONLY

DATE _May 18_  19 --

SIGN HERE FOR LESS CASH RECEIVED

**Midtown Bank**
Dallas, Texas

⑈⑆10000 20⑆:  ⑆⑆56 1386 2⑈

---

**MELINDA OR CLARENCE CRAMER**
7750 GRUBB DRIVE
DALLAS, TEXAS 75149

0783  VI-41
32-866/1110

May 14  19 --

PAY TO THE ORDER OF _Dewey E. Scott_  $850.00

_Eight hundred fifty and_ no/100 ———— DOLLARS

FOR CLASSROOM USE ONLY

**D**ALLAS **C**OUNTY
**C**REDIT **U**NION   Dallas, Texas

_Clarence Cramer_

FOR _Rent - condo_

⑈⑆100866⑆:⑆0783⑆765532 45⑈

ENDORSE HERE

Dewey Scott

DO NOT WRITE, STAMP OR SIGN BELOW THIS LINE
RESERVED FOR FINANCIAL INSTITUTION USE.

*FEDERAL RESERVE BOARD OF GOVERNORS REG. CC

Please List Each Check Separately

| CHECKS | DOLLARS | CENTS |
|---|---|---|
| 1 | | |
| 2 | | |
| 3 | | |
| 4 | | |
| 5 | | |
| 6 | | |
| 7 | | |
| 8 | | |
| 9 | | |
| 10 | | |
| 11 | | |
| 12 | | |
| 13 | | |
| 14 | | |
| 15 | | |
| 16 | | |
| TOTAL THIS SIDE ENTER THIS TOTAL ON REVERSE SIDE | | |

*FEDERAL RESERVE BOARD OF GOVERNORS REG. CC

*FEDERAL RESERVE BOARD OF GOVERNORS REG. CC

*FEDERAL RESERVE BOARD OF GOVERNORS REG. CC

DO NOT WRITE, STAMP OR SIGN BELOW THIS LINE
RESERVED FOR FINANCIAL INSTITUTION USE.

DO NOT WRITE, STAMP OR SIGN BELOW THIS LINE
RESERVED FOR FINANCIAL INSTITUTION USE.

DO NOT WRITE, STAMP OR SIGN BELOW THIS LINE
RESERVED FOR FINANCIAL INSTITUTION USE.

ENDORSE HERE
Dewey E. Scott

ENDORSE HERE
Trinity River Realtors
Acct. 4563815

ENDORSE HERE
Trinity River Realtors
Acct. 4563815